30-Minute KETOGENIC COOKING

Kyndra D. Holley

Victory Belt Publishing Inc.
Las Vegas

I dedicate this book to my readers. Without all of you, none of this would be possible. Your love and support mean more than you could ever know. Thank you for putting your trust and belief in me. We are all in this together!

First Published in 2018 by Victory Belt Publishing Inc.

Copyright © 2018 Kyndra D. Holley

ISBN-13: 978-1-628602-78-4

Front and Back Cover Photography by Hayley Mason and Bill Staley

Interior Design by Charisse Reyes

Printed in Canada

TC 0418

Table of Contents

Hey, friends!

I am so excited to share this book with you. *30-Minute Ketogenic Cooking* is going to show you how you can be eating delicious real-food, low-carb recipes with just 30 minutes of hands-on cooking time or less.

I am the type of person who likes to provide solutions to common, everyday struggles. One of the concerns I have heard the most from people trying to stick to a low-carb, ketogenic lifestyle is that they don't have enough time—not enough time for meal prep, not enough time for cooking, not enough time for family, not enough time for a social life, and so on. As a society, we are more rushed than ever, and we seem to be chasing this imaginary clock that is counting down at a breakneck pace. While I can't add more hours to any given day, I *can* subtract some of the time you spend in the kitchen, freeing up that time for things you would rather be doing.

Not only do I provide you with more than 50 quick-and-easy recipes, but I am also going to show you how you can save a lot of time by using the right kitchen tools and appliances, give you tips for meal prepping, and even share some creative ways to repurpose leftovers.

Cooking does not have to be a daunting task; in fact, it can be a joyous time once you get a system down that works for you. Many of our fondest memories in life are tied to food, and with those memories come very strong emotions. Maybe it is the thought of your grandma's home-baked apple pie or the delicious aromas of a slow-cooked meal shared with loved ones. If time is your issue in the kitchen, then my hope is that this book will help you find the joy in cooking again, while also providing you with more free time.

Peace and love,

Cooking is one of the strongest ceremonies for life. When recipes are put together, the kitchen is a chemical laboratory involving air, fire, water and the earth. This is what gives value to humans and elevates their spiritual qualities. If you take a frozen box and stick it in the microwave, you become connected to the factory.

—*Laura Esquivel*

Part 1
RESOURCES

Products Used in This Book

In this section, I highlight some of the items that you will see frequently throughout this book. I make it my mission to use only easy-to-find, real-food ingredients. You won't find anything in *30-Minute Ketogenic Cooking* that you wouldn't be able to buy at your local grocery store. My goal is to make sticking to a low-carb, ketogenic lifestyle as easy as possible. I have highlighted some of my favorite tried-and-true brands for you. As the keto diet grows in popularity, new products and brands are popping up all the time. It can lead to a lot of confusion and a sense of analysis paralysis when trying to decide which products are the best and will provide the best nutritional value. I hope this section will help take some of the guesswork out of it for you so that you can keep calm and keto on!

ALMOND FLOUR—I use finely ground blanched almond flour. A couple of my favorite brands are Bob's Red Mill and Anthony's.

APPLE CIDER VINEGAR—When selecting a brand of apple cider vinegar, look for a raw, unfiltered version with the "mother." My favorite brand is Bragg.

AVOCADO OIL—Avocado oil is easily my favorite cooking oil. I use it for nearly everything. It is right up there with butter for me. Refined avocado oil has a smoke point of over 500°F, making it excellent for high-temperature cooking and frying. It also has a very light and neutral flavor, making it great for salad dressings and homemade mayo.

BACON—Not all bacon is created equal. In fact, many brands of bacon are loaded with multiple forms of sugar. You might be not-so-pleasantly surprised when you read the labels. Some of my favorite sugar-free, clean-ingredient brands are Fletcher's, Hempler's, and Pederson's Natural Farms.

BROTH AND STOCK—Making your own bone broth and stock is a lot easier than it might sound. It is also very cost-effective and a great way to take a "waste not, want not" approach to cooking. I am all about reducing waste whenever possible. The added bonus is that homemade bone broth is rich in minerals to help support a healthy immune system. It also contains gut-healing compounds like collagen, glutamine, glycine, and proline. That being said, it is perfectly fine to go the stock-in-a-box route. However, be sure to scour the labels and look for a brand that is organic and contains no added sugars. The only ingredients should be water, chicken or beef, vegetables, spices, salt, and vinegar.

BUTTER—I use grass-fed butter for just about everything. Cooking in butter is one of my favorite ways to add a boost of healthy fat and major flavor to meals. For the recipes in this book, I used unsalted butter unless otherwise noted.

COCONUT AMINOS—The Spicy Sausage and Cabbage Stir-Fry recipe in this book calls for either coconut aminos or gluten-free soy sauce. Personally, I use coconut aminos in place of soy sauce for just about everything. My preferred brands are Coconut Secret and Trader Joe's. If you're going to use soy sauce, be sure to look for a gluten-free version, such as tamari.

COCONUT FLOUR—In my recipes, I use finely ground coconut flour. The brand I use most frequently is Nutiva.

ERYTHRITOL (GRANULAR, POWDERED, AND BROWN SUGAR)—The sweet recipes in this book, and even a couple of the savory recipes, call for granular, powdered, or brown sugar erythritol. The two brands that I use regularly and highly recommend are Swerve and LC Foods Company. Ordering online from LC Foods Company will likely save you a few dollars. LC is my go-to for brown sugar erythritol.

MEATS—Whenever possible, I purchase grass-fed, organic, and pastured meats from local family farms. It is important to me to know the history of my meat and to support companies that put the ethical treatment of animals at the forefront of their mission, vision, and values. Buying local also lowers my carbon footprint.

PASTURED EGGS—Buying pastured eggs from local farms is very important to me. Not only does it support my local economy, but farm-fresh eggs are healthier and less expensive than factory-farmed eggs from the grocery store. Why would I spend more money for an inferior product? Seems like a no-brainer to me. Pastured eggs have beautifully creamy deep orange yolks and are much higher in omega-3 fatty acids and vitamin E. The difference in color and taste is remarkable. Once you eat a farm-fresh egg, there is no going back. Most importantly, I refuse to support factory farming practices. Happy chickens lay happy eggs, and I love happy animals.

SPICES AND SEASONINGS—My favorite store-bought brand of spices and seasonings is Simply Organic. I typically buy them on Amazon to get the best deal. I also buy organic spices in the bulk section of my local grocery store.

SUGAR-FREE DARK CHOCOLATE CHIPS—A few of the recipes in this book call for sugar-free dark chocolate chips. My favorite brand is Lily's. They are sweetened with stevia and don't have any strange and unnecessary ingredients. LC Foods Company also makes great low-carb chocolate chips.

Time-Saving Kitchen Tips and Tricks

ORGANIZATION AND EFFICIENCY

 KEEP A RUNNING SHOPPING LIST. Keep it stuck to the fridge, on the inside of a kitchen cupboard, or even on the notepad app on your phone. Keeping a running list and adding things to it immediately upon running out will make it so that you always know what you need from the grocery store. You won't have to go searching through the fridge and pantry before shopping or make any last-minute store runs for just one or two ingredients.

 STICK TO YOUR LIST. It can be so easy to stray from your grocery list once you get to the store, especially if you are shopping on an empty stomach and hunger strikes. Before you leave to go shopping, take your running list and your meal plan for the week and compile a list of exactly what you need. Don't deviate from that list. Not only will getting just the things you need save you money, but your groceries will be a lot easier to put away when you get home.

 SIGN UP FOR GROCERY DELIVERY. Many grocery stores offer delivery for free or for a nominal fee. I was skeptical at first, until I tried it. They get my order right every time, the prices are the same as they are in the store, and the delivery person even brings the bags inside for me. Grocery delivery is a huge time-saver, and I even get to use my store rewards just as I would in-store.

 ASK THE MEAT AND SEAFOOD DEPARTMENTS FOR HELP. Ask them to package meat in smaller portions or to trim meat for you. You can also ask them to peel and devein shrimp, portion and cut fish, and so on. Having some of these tasks done for you will reduce your overall prep and cooking time dramatically.

 KEEP YOUR CABINETS, FRIDGE, AND PANTRY ORGANIZED. Keeping your kitchen organized is the key to preventing food waste, not buying unneeded items, and not feeling stressed out every time you set out to cook a meal. Before you go grocery shopping, take stock of what is in your fridge and get rid of any old or expired food. Do the same with your pantry. We all have that random canned good that has been in the pantry for years longer than we care to admit. Rotate the food in your pantry, placing the items with the earliest expiration dates in front. Make sure that the labels are facing forward so you can see at a glance what you have on hand. Go through your food storage containers and discard any pieces that are old or damaged or no longer have lids.

READ RECIPES IN FULL. Before you start cooking, read each recipe in its entirety to ensure that you have all the necessary ingredients and tools to prepare it. It's no fun to get halfway through a recipe only to realize that you do not have enough of a specific ingredient or do not have the right tools for the job. Also, be sure to take note of cooking times, marinating or chilling times, and resting times to ensure that you give yourself enough time to complete the recipe.

 CLEAN AS YOU GO. I am a firm believer that physical clutter equates to mental clutter, and for me, it really adds up. I can't have an enjoyable, stress-free time in the kitchen if there are dirty dishes piled everywhere and ingredients spread across every countertop. Not to mention, how would anyone find cooking enjoyable when afterward the kitchen looks like a bomb exploded? You can do a lot of little things as you cook to keep your space clean and reduce the overall amount of time spent in the kitchen. First, use a garbage bowl—a dedicated bowl on the counter that serves as a catchall for food scraps, empty packaging, or anything you might throw away at the end. Then, when you are finished, you can empty it all at once instead of having garbage spread everywhere. Second, load the dishwasher as you go. Instead of putting all the pots, pans, plates, and utensils you used to prepare the meal in the sink for later, rinse them and load them into the dishwasher as you finish with them. Third, keep a nontoxic cleaner and a towel on the counter and clean the countertops as you go, wiping up spills along the way. Finally, put away ingredients as you use them. For example, if you need one rib of chopped celery, grab just that one rib and put the rest of the celery away immediately. Not only does this reduce clutter on the counter, but it also means less work after mealtime is over.

 USE THE RIGHT UTENSILS FOR THE JOB. It might sound like a no-brainer, but I can't tell you how many times I have seen people pull out a slotted spoon for soups, stews, or sauces. Just like you wouldn't use a fork to cut your steak, you aren't going to use a saucepan to fry eggs.

 UTILIZE SLOW COOKERS AND PRESSURE COOKERS. Taking advantage of appliances that do most of the work for you is a huge time-saver. These appliances allow you to "set it and forget it," so to speak. Another great thing about slow cookers and pressure cookers is their large capacity, which allows you to double or triple a recipe and have leftovers for meal prep. They also make for far fewer dirty dishes.

 GET OTHERS INVOLVED IN THE COOKING PROCESS. This will help reduce your prep time and will make the experience of creating healthy meals a family affair. Assign older children a night of the week to contribute in the kitchen and teach them to cook something simple yet enjoyable.

✓ **COOK ONCE AND EAT TWICE.** I always practice this method. I cook more than we need for just one meal so that we can have leftovers and always have a running stock of healthy prepared food on hand—perfect for weekday lunches or busy weeknights when I just can't stand the thought of cooking dinner when I get home.

MEAL PREP AND PLANNING

(1) **BUY VEGETABLES IN BULK WHEN THEY ARE ON SALE.** Then cut them down to the most frequently used sizes—dice, chop, julienne, and so on. Freeze them in individual portions for later. This trick will save you so much time, and shopping according to the sales will save you money.

(2) **PREP YOUR INGREDIENTS BEFORE YOU BEGIN COOKING.** Slice, chop, dice, and measure ingredients in advance. Then you will have everything ready to go for each step of the recipe.

(3) **PORTION OUT THE INGREDIENTS YOU USE FREQUENTLY, SUCH AS STOCK, SAUCES, COOKING FATS, AND HERBS.** Ice cube trays are terrific for this task. You can freeze individual cubes of stock, and then you'll always have it on hand. Ice cube trays are also great for freezing fresh herbs in olive oil or avocado oil. Freeze combinations that you frequently use on proteins, like garlic and rosemary for steak or chicken. Making large batches of sauces and freezing them in individual portions is another great time-saver.

(4) **BATCH COOK MEAT FOR LATER USE IN RECIPES.** Roast whole chickens and then break them down and portion out the meat. This would be perfect for Buffalo Chicken Roasted Cabbage Steaks (page 102). Grill or broil large batches of meat on your outdoor grill or on a sheet pan and then portion it out and freeze it for later. Make a large batch of ground meat, season it with Taco Seasoning (page 138), and freeze it for a quick-and-easy reheat on the next Taco Tuesday. Cook large batches of bacon and chop it for later use—perfect for adding to recipes or as a topper for salads.

(5) **DON'T BE AFRAID TO UTILIZE FROZEN VEGETABLES.** While fresh vegetables are always best, you can usually save a little time and money by keeping a good stock of frozen organic vegetables on hand.

6   **HARD-BOIL A DOZEN EGGS AT A TIME.** I always have hard-boiled eggs in my fridge. They are perfect for quick snacks, making deviled eggs, or adding to recipes.

7   **HAVE THE TOOLS YOU NEED ON HAND.** The proper storage containers, freezer bags, and so on make meal prep much more efficient.

8   **SET ASIDE TIME EACH WEEK FOR MEAL PREP.** Schedule this time as you would a job. Devoting two to three hours on Sunday morning can save you significant time during the week. Getting all the prep work done in one day frees up your time during the week, and you can relax knowing that you have a stockpile of healthy food on hand.

9   **OVERLAP INGREDIENTS ACROSS MULTIPLE RECIPES.** This will save you both time and money in the kitchen. If mushrooms are on sale this week, for example, cut them all down at the same time and plan recipes for the week that include mushrooms.

10   **COOK MULTIPLE FOODS AT THE SAME TIME WHENEVER POSSIBLE.** One of my favorite ways to do this is with sheet pan meals. I throw my protein and vegetables on a rimmed baking sheet and cook them all together. Dinner doesn't get much simpler than that!

Time-Saving Kitchen Tools and Appliances

There are a lot of things you can do to save yourself time in the kitchen, and perhaps topping the list is having the right tools for the job. In this section, I outline some of my favorite kitchen tools and appliances and detail exactly how they will save you time and effort.

BENCH SCRAPER—Traditionally used for dough, a bench scraper is the perfect scoop for chopped and diced ingredients. It makes transferring prepped ingredients from a cutting board into a pan a cinch.

BLENDER—The blender might be one of the most underutilized kitchen appliances—a high-powered blender, that is. I managed to blow the motor out on several cheap blenders before taking the plunge and buying a Vitamix. It was only then that I realized what a blender can really do, from making soups and sauces to whipping up pancake batter or scrambled eggs. I even use it for making whipped cream and grinding nuts. A high-powered blender is definitely a must-have for me.

BOX GRATER—A four-sided box grater isn't just for cheese; it is also great for grating vegetables. This is perhaps one of the least expensive but most effective kitchen tools you can buy.

ELECTRIC PRESSURE COOKER—The electric pressure cooker, especially the Instant Pot (which also performs other functions), is rapidly increasing in popularity, and for good reason. Unlike the exploding stovetop pressure cookers of the seventies, today's electric pressure cookers are much safer and a lot more user-friendly. A pressure cooker gives you the ability to make a recipe that would normally take hours in mere minutes.

EXTRA-LARGE SKILLET—My oversized 17-inch ovenproof skillet is one of my absolute favorite items in my kitchen. It's perfect for extra-large one-pot meals, meal prep, batch cooking, and doubling and tripling recipes to feed a lot of people.

FOOD PROCESSOR—A high-end food processor can replace multiple kitchen gadgets, providing a time-saving, all-in-one solution. A food processor is also an amazing space saver for small kitchens. This one simple appliance can make slicing, chopping, shredding, and grating large quantities of food quick and easy. It also contains the mess, making for easier cleanup.

IMMERSION BLENDER—I'm honestly not sure how I managed to cook for so many years without an immersion blender. It is easily in my top five when it comes to time-saving kitchen tools. It gives you the ability to puree anything right in the pot or pan it was cooked in. This means no more transferring hot foods, which means a lot less spillage and fewer dirty dishes. It is also instrumental for me in making homemade mayo. You can find my 2-Minute Mayo recipe in my book *Craveable Keto,* as well as on my website, peaceloveandlowcarb.com.

KITCHEN SHEARS—Most knife blocks come with a pair of kitchen shears. In fact, you may have a pair sitting in your block right now, just waiting to be used. There is not a day I spend in the kitchen when the shears don't come out to play. I use them for snipping herbs, trimming low-carb dough, cutting bacon, and even cutting and deboning poultry. Shears are also handy for hard-to-open food packaging.

MANDOLINE SLICER—A mandoline makes the task of slicing vegetables a breeze. Most brands come with multiple blades, giving you the ability to make several different cuts— slices, wedges, julienne, and so on. Just be careful not to lose a finger, as mandolines are razor sharp.

OVENPROOF SKILLETS—Being able to start a recipe on the stovetop and then transfer it to the oven without having to heat and then dirty another pan is a great time-saver. My favorite materials for this purpose are cast iron, enameled cast iron, and stainless steel. Lodge and Calphalon are two of my favorite pan makers.

PREP CONTAINERS—Buying a set of prep containers in varying sizes is like investing in your future time-saving efforts. These containers are great for prepping ingredients that you use frequently, like onions, peppers, and cheese, in bulk so that you don't have to prep them for each meal, and also for storing leftovers.

RIMMED BAKING SHEETS—If there was one theme throughout all of my books and recipes, it would likely be rimmed baking sheets. I am the queen of easy cleanup, so rimmed baking sheets are an integral part of my everyday kitchen routine. The rimmed sides prevent spillage, they make a great surface for less-than-stable cookware, such as silicone bakeware, and they only get better with age. A well-loved baking sheet is almost as amazing as a perfectly seasoned cast-iron pan. Best of all, rimmed baking sheets are easy to clean, especially when you line them with parchment paper or a silicone baking mat like I do in many of my recipes.

RUBBER SPATULA—I love any tool or gadget that serves more than one function. I use a rubber spatula just about every time I cook—mix, stir, and scrape all in one.

SILICONE BAKEWARE—In addition to my deep love affair with silicone baking mats (see below), I love silicone bakeware in general. Have you ever made meatloaf in a loaf pan or a batch of muffins in a muffin pan only to spend longer cleaning the pan than it took you to make the recipe? Yeah, me, too! But not with silicone bakeware—nothing sticks to it.

SILICONE BAKING MATS—Silicone baking mats, oh, how I love thee. I would like to meet the person who created them and give that person an awkwardly long hug. Long gone are the days of cooking on aluminum foil. Not only do silicone baking mats cook foods evenly, but they are about the easiest things to clean imaginable. Nothing, and I mean *nothing*, sticks to them. Best of all, they are reusable, so you aren't spending money on something you are going to use once and then throw away.

SLOW COOKER—Although "slow" implies that it takes longer, which it does, the wonderful thing about a slow cooker is that it does all the work for you. Instead of spending all that time in the kitchen, you can spend your time doing the things you love while the slow cooker works its magic.

STAND MIXER—While not a necessity, a stand mixer sure is a great convenience. It does the mixing for you while you work on other steps of a recipe.

Repurposing Leftovers

Repurposing leftovers is hands down my favorite way to cut down on time spent in the kitchen. I've come up with some pretty creative dishes that have ended up becoming family favorites. Here are some of my best tips and tricks for giving those leftovers a second time in the spotlight.

SOUP—Not only is soup one of my all-time favorite foods, but it is a great way to use up leftover vegetables. Whether it's leftover Sautéed Asparagus with Mushrooms and Bacon (page 114) or leftover sautéed or roasted vegetables from yesterday's dinner, you can pour them into a pot with some stock and a protein and you are all set.

BONE BROTH—If you roasted an entire chicken or turkey and aren't sure what to do with the small amount of meat that is left on the carcass, throw the entire thing into a slow cooker or Dutch oven with some garlic, onion, celery, carrots, apple cider vinegar, and spices, such as oregano, rosemary, basil, and thyme, and simmer low and slow to create a rich, nutrient-dense broth.

STIR-FRY—Take leftover meat and vegetables, toss them into a wok or high-sided frying pan, add some coconut aminos, rice vinegar, and toasted sesame oil, and turn your leftovers into a delicious stir-fry.

FRIDGE DUMP PASTA—You might be amazed by the flavor combinations you can build by adding leftovers to some spiral-sliced veggies and a little marinara or a good garlic cream sauce. Turn last night's casserole into tonight's pasta dish!

SALAD—Perhaps the quickest and easiest way to use up leftovers is to slap them on a salad. Leftover meats and veggies can turn a side salad into a full meal deal.

BREAKFAST—Using leftovers in an omelet or scramble the next morning is a perfect way to make a delicious breakfast. You can even have breakfast for dinner. In our house, we call it "brinner."

WRAP IT UP—A good low-carb, gluten-free tortilla or even lettuce cups can turn dinner leftovers into the perfect lunch wrap.

TACO TUESDAY—Leftover steak or chicken can easily be turned into tacos, fajitas, burrito bowls, or even a taco salad. Just toss it in Taco Seasoning (page 138) and you are halfway there.

PUT AN EGG ON IT—As I have talked about in my other books, I am a big fan of the whole "put an egg on it" culture. Sometimes repurposing leftovers is as simple as adding an egg to dinner and calling it breakfast.

Weekly Meal Plans with Grocery Shopping Lists

WEEK 1 MEAL PLAN	DAY 1	DAY 2	DAY 3	
BREAKFAST	Ham and Cheese Waffles *8 servings*	Chicken Cordon Bleu Frittata *6 servings*	Ham and Cheese Waffles *Leftovers*	
LUNCH	Cucumber Dill Tuna Salad *4 servings*	Cheesy Salsa Verde Chicken Casserole *Leftovers*	Greek Meatballs *Leftovers*	
DINNER	Cheesy Salsa Verde Chicken Casserole *8 servings*	Greek Meatballs *6 servings*	Pork Chops with Herbed Goat Cheese Butter *4 servings*	
SALAD OR SIDE	Green Onion and Lime Cauliflower Rice *6 servings*	Green Onion and Lime Cauliflower Rice *Leftovers*	Herbed Goat Cheese and Cauliflower Mash *8 servings*	
DESSERT OR SNACK	Avocado Chocolate Pudding *4 servings*	Chocolate Chip Cookies for Two	Double Chocolate Flourless Brownies *16 servings*	

	DAY 4	DAY 5	DAY 6	DAY 7
	Cheesy Pico Eggs *1 serving—make as many servings as needed* **64**	Sausage Balls *6 servings* **66**	Ham and Spinach Eggs Benedict *4 servings* **62**	Sour Cream and Chive Egg Clouds *4 servings* **68**
	Fish Taco Bowls *4 servings* **92**	Taco Wedge Salad *4 servings* **72**	Barbecue Chicken Mockaroni Salad *8 servings* **56**	Zucchini Noodles with Hamburger Gravy *Leftovers* **80**
	Skillet Chicken Parmesan *4 servings* **96**	Grilled New York Strip Steak with Blue Cheese Dijon Cream Sauce *4 servings* **90**	Zucchini Noodles with Hamburger Gravy *6 servings* **80**	Herbed Chicken with Mushrooms *4 servings* **94**
	Shaved Brussels Sprouts and Kale Salad *8 servings* **48**	Sautéed Asparagus with Mushrooms and Bacon *4 servings* **114**	Shaved Brussels Sprouts and Kale Salad *Leftovers* **48**	Cheesy Zucchini Gratin *8 servings* **112**
	Double Chocolate Flourless Brownies *Leftovers* **128**	Buttery Garlic Crescent Rolls *12 servings* **38**	Lemon Mousse *6 servings* **130**	Buttery Garlic Crescent Rolls *Leftovers* **38**

WEEK 1 SHOPPING LIST

DAIRY/EGGS
butter, 2 pounds

cream cheese, 1 block

crumbled blue cheese, 1 container

crumbled feta cheese, 1 container

eggs, 4 dozen

goat cheese, 1 log

grated Parmesan cheese, 1 container

heavy cream, 2 quarts

mascarpone cheese, 1 container

sharp cheddar cheese, 1 large block

sharp white cheddar cheese, 1 block

shredded low-moisture, part-skim mozzarella cheese, 1 large package

sliced Swiss cheese, 1 package

sour cream, 1 pint

MEAT/POULTRY/SEAFOOD
bacon, 2 packages

boneless, skinless chicken breasts, 4½ pounds

bulk Italian sausage, 1 pound

Canadian bacon or thinly sliced ham, 8 ounces

ground beef, 4 pounds

ham, 1 pound

New York strip steaks, 4 (8 ounces each)

thick-cut boneless pork loin chops, 4 (about 2 pounds total)

wild-caught cod or halibut, 1½ pounds

STAPLES/CONDIMENTS/SPICES
apple cider vinegar, 1 bottle

baking powder

baking soda

blanched almond flour, 1 package

cayenne pepper

celery salt

chicken stock, 1 quart

chili powder

cocoa powder, 1 container

coconut flour, 1 package

Dijon mustard, 1 bottle

dried minced onions

dried oregano

dried rubbed sage

garlic powder

granular erythritol, 1 package

ground cinnamon

ground cumin

ground nutmeg

Italian seasoning

liquid smoke, 1 bottle

mayonnaise, 1 jar

mustard powder

olive oil, 1 bottle

onion powder

peanut butter powder, 1 package (see page 128)

powdered erythritol, 1 package

prepared yellow mustard, 1 bottle

pure vanilla extract, 1 bottle

red pepper flakes

sugar-free dark chocolate chips, 1 package

white vinegar, 1 bottle

FRESH PRODUCE

asparagus, 1 pound

avocados, 5

basil, 1 package

Brussels sprouts, 1 pound

cauliflower, 5 large heads

celery, 1 bunch

cherry tomatoes, 1 package

chives, 2 bundles

cilantro, 1 bunch

dill, 1 package

flat-leaf parsley, 1 bundle

garlic, 5 bulbs

green cabbage, 1 head

green onions, 1 bunch

iceberg lettuce, 1 head

jalapeño peppers, 2

lacinato kale, 1 bunch

lemons, 3

limes, 2

mini seedless cucumber, 1

mint, 1 package

mushrooms, 8 ounces

red bell pepper, 1

red cabbage, 1 head

red onion, 1

rosemary, 1 package

small onions, 4

spinach leaves, 8 cups

thyme, 1 package

tomatoes, 3

yellow bell pepper, 1

zucchini, 4 large and 4 medium

CANNED/JARRED GOODS

black olives, 1 can

coconut milk, 1 can

creamy almond butter, 1 jar

dill pickle relish, 1 jar

dill pickles, 1 jar

marinara sauce, 1 jar

salsa verde, 1 jar (or ingredients to make homemade, page 139)

sustainably caught tuna, 2 (5-ounce) cans

tomato sauce, 1 can

WEEK 2 MEAL PLAN	DAY 1	DAY 2	DAY 3	
BREAKFAST	Cheesy Pico Eggs *1 serving—make as many servings as needed* **64**	Chicken Cordon Bleu Frittata *6 servings* **72**	Fortune Cookie Waffles *8 servings* **60**	
LUNCH	Fish Taco Bowls *4 servings* **92**	Cucumber Dill Tuna Salad *4 servings* **54**	Chicken Sausage and Vegetable Skillet *Leftovers* **82**	
DINNER	Buffalo Chicken Roasted Cabbage Steaks *6 servings* **102**	Chicken Sausage and Vegetable Skillet *6 servings* **82**	Zucchini Noodles with Pesto Cream Sauce *4 servings* **104**	
SALAD OR SIDE	Sautéed Asparagus with Mushrooms and Bacon *4 servings* **114**	Sautéed Green Beans with Ham *6 servings* **118**	Shaved Brussels Sprouts and Kale Salad *8 servings* **48**	
DESSERT OR SNACK	Sesame Shortbread Sugar Cookies *12 servings* **132**	Cheddar Jalapeño Bacon Biscuits *8 servings* **42**	Sesame Shortbread Sugar Cookies *Leftovers* **132**	

DAY 4	DAY 5	DAY 6	DAY 7
62	60	66	68
Ham and Spinach Eggs Benedict *4 servings*	Fortune Cookie Waffles *Leftovers*	Sausage Balls *6 servings*	Sour Cream and Chive Egg Clouds *4 servings*
52	46	78	86
Taco Wedge Salad *4 servings*	Strawberry Spinach Salad *4 servings*	Spicy Sausage and Cabbage Stir-Fry *Leftovers*	Cheesy Salsa Verde Chicken Casserole *Leftovers*
78	98	86	100
Spicy Sausage and Cabbage Stir-Fry *6 servings*	Shrimp Piccata *4 servings*	Cheesy Salsa Verde Chicken Casserole *8 servings*	Salisbury Steak *4 servings*
48	108	110	56
Shaved Brussels Sprouts and Kale Salad *Leftovers*	Pan-Fried Brussels Sprouts with Creamy Dijon Cider Dressing *8 servings*	Green Onion and Lime Cauliflower Rice *6 servings*	Barbecue Chicken Mockaroni Salad *8 servings*
42	36	32	124
Cheddar Jalapeño Bacon Biscuits *Leftovers*	Dill Pickle Deviled Eggs *6 servings*	Buffalo Chicken Dip *8 servings*	Chocolate Chip Cookies for Two

WEEK 2 SHOPPING LIST

DAIRY/EGGS
butter, 1 pound
cream cheese, 4 blocks
crumbled blue cheese, 1 container
crumbled feta cheese, 1 container
eggs, 4 dozen
heavy cream, 1 quart
sharp cheddar cheese, 1 large block
shredded low-moisture, part-skim mozzarella cheese, 1 large package
shredded Parmesan cheese, 1 container
sliced Swiss cheese, 1 package
sour cream, 1 pint

MEAT/POULTRY/SEAFOOD
bacon, 3 packages
boneless, skinless chicken breasts, 4½ pounds
bulk Italian sausage, 1 pound
Canadian bacon, 8 ounces
chicken sausage links, 5
extra-large shrimp (26/30), 1 pound
ground beef, 2½ pounds
ham, 1 pound
hot bulk Italian sausage, 1 pound
rotisserie chicken, 1
wild-caught cod or halibut, 1½ pounds

STAPLES/CONDIMENTS/SPICES
apple cider vinegar, 1 bottle
baking powder
beef bouillon granules or cubes, 1 container
beef stock, 1 quart
blanched almond flour, 1 package
Buffalo wing sauce, 1 bottle
cayenne pepper
celery salt
chicken stock, 1 quart
chili powder
coconut aminos, 1 bottle
coconut flour, 1 package
Dijon mustard, 1 bottle
dried minced onions
garlic powder
granular erythritol, 1 package
ground cumin
hot sauce, 1 bottle
Italian seasoning
liquid smoke, 1 bottle
mayonnaise, 1 jar
mustard powder
olive oil, 1 bottle
onion powder
powdered erythritol, 1 package
prepared yellow mustard, 1 bottle
pure vanilla extract, 1 bottle
red pepper flakes
reduced-sugar ketchup, 1 bottle
roasted and salted pecan halves, 1 package
sugar-free dark chocolate chips, 1 package
toasted sesame oil, 1 bottle
toasted sesame seeds, 1 jar
toasted walnuts, 1 package
unseasoned rice vinegar, 1 bottle
white vinegar, 1 bottle
Worcestershire sauce, 1 bottle

FRESH PRODUCE

asparagus, 1 pound

avocados, 3

baby arugula, 1 bunch

basil, 1 package

Brussels sprouts, 3 pounds

cauliflower, 3 large heads

celery, 1 bunch

cherry tomatoes, 2 packages

chives, 2 bundles

cilantro, 1 bunch

cremini mushrooms, 1½ pounds

dill, 1 package

flat-leaf parsley, 1 bunch

garlic, 3 bulbs

gingerroot, 1

green beans, 1 pound

green bell pepper, 1 small

green cabbage, 1 large head

green onions, 1 bunch

iceberg lettuce, 1 head

jalapeño pepper, 1

lacinato kale, 1 bunch

lemons, 4

limes, 4

mini seedless cucumber, 1

napa cabbage, 1 head

onions, 3 small

red bell peppers, 2 small

red cabbage, 1 head

red onions, 3 small

spinach leaves, 3 bags

strawberries, 1 small container

vine-ripened tomatoes, 2

yellow bell pepper, 1

yellow squash, 1 small

zucchini, 3 large

CANNED/JARRED GOODS

black olives, 1 can

capers, 1 jar

dill pickles, 1 jar

pesto, 1 jar

pickle relish, 1 jar

pickled jalapeño peppers, 1 jar

salsa verde, 1 jar (or ingredients to make homemade, page 139)

sun-dried tomatoes, 1 jar

sustainably caught tuna, 2 (5-ounce) cans

tahini, 1 jar

tomato sauce, 1 (8-ounce) can

Cooking is like painting or writing a song.
Just as there are only so many notes or colors,
there are only so many flavors—it's how you
combine them that sets you apart.

—*Wolfgang Puck*

Part 2
RECIPES

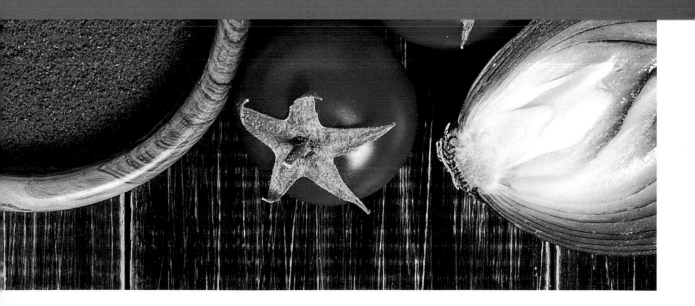

STARTERS
AND
Snacks

Buffalo Chicken Dip / 32

Mediterranean Flatbread / 34

Dill Pickle Deviled Eggs / 36

Buttery Garlic Crescent Rolls / 38

Tahini Ranch Dip / 40

Pico de Gallo / 41

Cheddar Jalapeño Bacon
Biscuits / 42

Buffalo Chicken Dip

   makes 8 servings · prep time: 10 minutes · cook time: 30 minutes

This dip is one of my favorite things to bring to any sort of potluck-style gathering or football party. It is always the first dish wiped clean. I like to serve it with sliced cucumbers and celery sticks. It is also really great served with cut up red bell peppers and pork rinds.

ingredients

1 pound boneless, skinless chicken breasts or thighs, cooked and chopped (see tip)

1 (8-ounce) package full-fat cream cheese, softened

¾ cup crumbled blue cheese, divided

½ cup shredded mozzarella cheese

¾ cup Buffalo wing sauce

¼ cup full-fat sour cream

2 cloves garlic, minced

1 large rib celery, chopped, divided

2 tablespoons chopped fresh chives, for garnish

directions

1. Preheat the oven to 375°F.

2. Place the chicken, cream cheese, ½ cup of the blue cheese crumbles, mozzarella, Buffalo sauce, sour cream, garlic, and half of the celery in a large mixing bowl. Mix until the ingredients are well incorporated.

3. Transfer the mixture to an 8-inch square baking dish. Bake for 30 minutes, or until the dip is heated all the way through and the top begins to bubble.

4. Serve in the baking dish or transfer to a serving bowl. Garnish with the remaining blue cheese and celery and the chives. Store leftovers in the refrigerator for up to 1 week.

time-saving tip:

You can make this recipe with rotisserie chicken to save time in the kitchen. Be sure to read the ingredient label, as many store-bought rotisserie chickens contain added sugar.

CALORIES: 230 | FAT: 16g | PROTEIN: 18g | TOTAL CARBS: 2.4g | DIETARY FIBER: 0.2g | NET CARBS: 2.2g

Mediterranean Flatbread

NET CARBS
3.8g

makes 8 servings · prep time: 10 minutes · cook time: 24 minutes

Just thinking about this flatbread makes my mouth water. In my high-carb, gluten-filled days, I used to eat a Mediterranean flatbread at a local restaurant. I ordered it every time we ate there. So when I began living a strict low-carb and gluten-free lifestyle, I just knew that I had to re-create that dish to suit the way I was eating, and that I did! I love to serve this flatbread with Avocado Ranch Dressing (page 142).

ingredients

¾ cup blanched almond flour

1 teaspoon garlic powder

1 teaspoon onion powder

1 teaspoon Italian seasoning

½ teaspoon sea salt

¼ teaspoon ground black pepper

1½ cups shredded low-moisture, part-skim mozzarella cheese

1½ ounces full-fat cream cheese (3 tablespoons), softened

1 large egg

2 tablespoons pesto

¼ cup pitted and halved Kalamata olives

¼ cup diced tomatoes

A few thin slices red onion

⅓ cup crumbled fresh (soft) goat cheese

5 fresh basil leaves, thinly sliced, for garnish

directions

1. Preheat the oven to 425°F. Line a rimmed baking sheet with parchment paper or a silicone baking mat.

2. Place the almond flour, garlic powder, onion powder, Italian seasoning, salt, and pepper in a medium mixing bowl. Mix until the ingredients are well incorporated.

3. Put the mozzarella and cream cheese in a large microwave-safe mixing bowl. Microwave for 1 minute. Stir to combine the cheeses, then microwave for 1 more minute.

4. Add the almond flour mixture and the egg to the melted cheeses and, using your hands, quickly mix until the ingredients are well incorporated. If the dough becomes too stringy and unworkable, simply put it back in the microwave for 30 seconds at a time to soften.

5. On the prepared baking sheet, spread the dough into a thin, even layer, covering the entire surface of the pan.

6. Par-bake the crust for 10 to 12 minutes, until golden brown. Check the flatbread periodically to make sure that it does not bubble up. Use a toothpick to pop any bubbles.

7. Remove the baking sheet from the oven and spread the pesto evenly across the entire flatbread. Top with the olives, tomatoes, onion slices, and goat cheese. Return to the oven and bake for 10 more minutes.

8. Top with the fresh basil before serving. Store leftovers in the refrigerator for up to 1 week. Reheat in the oven at 250°F until warmed.

CALORIES: 201 | FAT: 16g | PROTEIN: 11g | TOTAL CARBS: 5.2g | DIETARY FIBER: 1.4g | NET CARBS: 3.8g

Dill Pickle Deviled Eggs

DAIRY-FREE · NUT-FREE · PALEO

NET CARBS
0.7g

makes 12 deviled eggs (2 per serving)
prep time: 10 minutes (not including time to boil eggs)

I am a huge fan of just about anything dill flavored. If you frequent my website or own any of my other books, then this will come as no surprise. Having hard-boiled eggs on hand at all times is one of my favorite ways to cut down on time spent in the kitchen. Hard-boiled eggs are also great for having something quick, easy, and healthy to grab when hunger hits.

ingredients

6 hard-boiled eggs (see tips), peeled

⅓ cup mayonnaise

3 tablespoons finely chopped dill pickles, plus extra for garnish

2 teaspoons chopped fresh dill weed, plus extra for garnish

1 teaspoon Dijon mustard

1 teaspoon dried minced onions

directions

1. Slice the eggs in half lengthwise and scoop the yolks into a medium mixing bowl. Mash the yolks with a fork. Set aside the whites.

2. Add the mayonnaise, pickles, dill, Dijon mustard, and dried onions to the bowl with the egg yolks. Mix until the ingredients are well combined.

3. Transfer the yolk mixture to a pastry bag or resealable plastic bag. If using a plastic bag, snip off one corner of the bag. Pipe the mixture into the egg whites.

4. Garnish each deviled egg with extra pickles and dill. Store leftovers in the refrigerator for up to 3 days.

tips: This is how I make perfect hard-boiled eggs: Place the eggs in a large saucepan with cold water. Add enough water so that the eggs are fully submerged. Over high heat, bring the water to a rolling boil. Once the water is boiling, remove the pan from the heat, cover, and let sit for 12 minutes. Submerge the eggs in a cold-water bath before peeling.

Making your own mayonnaise will not only save you money, but it is a lot healthier for you, too. Check out my 2-Minute Mayo recipe on peaceloveandlowcarb.com.

CALORIES: 147 | FAT: 13g | PROTEIN: 6g | TOTAL CARBS: 0.7g | DIETARY FIBER: 0g | NET CARBS: 0.7g

Buttery Garlic Crescent Rolls

NET CARBS
3.6g

makes 12 rolls (1 per serving) · prep time: 10 minutes · cook time: 27 minutes

How can you go wrong with light, fluffy, buttery crescent rolls? These are perfect to serve with breakfast, lunch, or dinner or even on their own.

ingredients

2 cups blanched almond flour

1 tablespoon baking powder

1½ teaspoons garlic powder, divided

1 teaspoon onion powder

3 cups shredded low-moisture, part-skim mozzarella cheese

2½ ounces full-fat cream cheese (5 tablespoons)

2 large eggs

2 tablespoons salted butter, melted

½ teaspoon Italian seasoning

directions

1. Preheat the oven to 425°F. Line a rimmed baking sheet with parchment paper or a silicone baking mat.

2. Put the almond flour, baking powder, 1 teaspoon of the garlic powder, and onion powder in a medium mixing bowl. Whisk until well combined; I like to put the mixture through a flour sifter to ensure that the baking powder gets fully mixed in with the rest of the ingredients.

3. Place the mozzarella and cream cheese in a large microwave-safe bowl. Microwave for 1 minute 30 seconds. Stir to combine the cheeses, then microwave for 1 more minute. Mix until the cheeses are well combined.

4. Add the almond flour mixture and the eggs to the melted cheeses. Using your hands, mix until the ingredients are well incorporated. If you are having a hard time mixing the ingredients together, put the bowl back in the microwave for another 20 to 30 seconds to soften. If the dough starts sticking to your hands, wet your hands slightly and continue working the dough.

5. Place the ball of dough between 2 pieces of parchment paper and roll it out into a 14-inch circle. Using a knife or pizza cutter, cut the circle into 12 equal wedges. Roll up each wedge, starting at the wide end and ending at the point, then place the rolls point side down on the prepared baking sheet.

6. Bake for 20 minutes, or until golden brown.

7. While the rolls are in the oven, combine the melted butter, Italian seasoning, and remaining ½ teaspoon of garlic powder. Remove the rolls from the oven, brush the tops with the butter mixture, and bake for an additional 5 minutes. Store leftovers in the refrigerator for up to 1 week. Reheat in the oven at 250°F until warmed.

CALORIES: 245 | FAT: 19g | PROTEIN: 14g | TOTAL CARBS: 5.6g | DIETARY FIBER: 2g | NET CARBS: 3.6g

Tahini Ranch Dip

 DAIRY-FREE · EGG-FREE · NUT-FREE · PALEO   makes 1½ cups (¼ cup per serving) · prep time: 10 minutes

This is one of my favorite dips to bring to summer get-togethers. It is almost always the first appetizer to go. It is fresh and light, but incredibly flavorful. I like to serve it with sliced bell peppers. It also makes a great salad dressing. A garnish of finely diced bell peppers makes for a pretty presentation.

ingredients

1 packed cup fresh spinach leaves

½ cup tahini

⅓ cup water

3 tablespoons chopped fresh dill weed

2 tablespoons chopped fresh chives

2 tablespoons apple cider vinegar

2 cloves garlic, peeled

¾ teaspoon sea salt

½ teaspoon onion powder

¼ teaspoon ground black pepper

directions

Place all of the ingredients in a blender or food processor and pulse until well incorporated. Store leftover dip in the refrigerator for up to 2 weeks.

CALORIES: 125 | FAT: 11g | PROTEIN: 5g | TOTAL CARBS: 3g | DIETARY FIBER: 1g | NET CARBS: 2g

Pico de Gallo

makes 2 cups (2 tablespoons per serving) · prep time: 15 minutes

Pico de gallo translates quite literally to "beak of rooster." While the origin of the term is not exactly clear, I can tell you that there are no rooster beaks in this recipe. Also called salsa fresca, traditional pico de gallo is simply chopped tomatoes, onions, fresh cilantro, some sort of hot pepper, and a little bit of lime juice. I put my own spin on things by adding fresh garlic. In my book, garlic makes everything better.

ingredients

2 vine-ripened tomatoes, seeded and finely chopped

1 jalapeño pepper, seeded and finely chopped

2 cloves garlic, minced

1 small onion, finely chopped (about ½ cup)

2 tablespoons chopped fresh cilantro

1 tablespoon fresh lime juice

¼ teaspoon sea salt

directions

Put all of the ingredients in a large mixing bowl and mix until well incorporated. Taste and add more salt, if desired. Store in the refrigerator for up to 1 week. Alternatively, you can freeze it for later use.

CALORIES: 7 | FAT: 0.3g | PROTEIN: 0.5g | TOTAL CARBS: 1.7g | DIETARY FIBER: 0.2g | NET CARBS: 1.5g

Cheddar Jalapeño Bacon Biscuits

NET CARBS
3.4g

makes 8 biscuits (1 per serving) · prep time: 10 minutes · cook time: 20 minutes

If there is a Red Lobster near you, then you already know how good their Cheddar Bay Biscuits are. However, they are not low-carb. So I knew that I needed to create my own healthier version to fit my low-carb lifestyle. I love to use these biscuits to make home-made biscuits and gravy or to serve with the Slow Cooker Kickin' Chili from my website, peaceloveandlowcarb.com.

ingredients

4 ounces full-fat cream cheese (½ cup), softened

1 large egg

1½ cups shredded sharp cheddar cheese

3 cloves garlic, minced

¼ teaspoon Italian seasoning

¼ teaspoon garlic powder

¼ teaspoon onion powder

1¼ cups blanched almond flour

¼ cup heavy cream

¼ cup water

6 slices bacon, cooked crisp and chopped

¼ cup chopped pickled jalapeño slices

directions

1. Preheat the oven to 350°F. Lightly grease 8 wells of a 12-well muffin top pan.

2. Beat the cream cheese and egg together with an electric hand mixer or a stand mixer until well combined.

3. Add the cheddar cheese, garlic, Italian seasoning, garlic powder, and onion powder and mix together using a rubber spatula.

4. Mix in the almond flour, heavy cream, and water. Fold the bacon and jalapeño slices into the dough.

5. Drop heaping mounds of the dough onto the prepared muffin top pan. Bake for 20 minutes, or until golden brown. Allow to cool in the pan before serving. Store leftovers in the refrigerator for up to 1 week.

tip: I recommend reheating leftover biscuits in a toaster oven; however, they are also pretty darn good cold.

CALORIES: 266 | FAT: 23g | PROTEIN: 12g | TOTAL CARBS: 5.4g | DIETARY FIBER: 2g | NET CARBS: 3.4g

Salads

Strawberry Spinach Salad / 46

Shaved Brussels Sprouts
and Kale Salad / 48

Greek Salad / 50

Taco Wedge Salad / 52

Cucumber Dill Tuna Salad / 54

Barbecue Chicken
Mockaroni Salad / 56

Strawberry Spinach Salad

 EGG-FREE

makes 4 servings · prep time: 15 minutes (not including time to cook bacon)

This salad goes into heavy rotation in my meal plan during the summer months, and I love that I can make it with strawberries from my own garden. To make it a full meal, I love to top it with blackened chicken or salmon. The combination of sweet, savory, and spicy is *ah-mazing!*

ingredients

4 packed cups fresh spinach leaves

8 strawberries, sliced

6 slices bacon, cooked crisp and chopped

½ cup crumbled feta cheese

⅓ cup toasted walnuts

A few thin slices red onion

Strawberry Balsamic Vinaigrette (page 143), for serving (optional)

directions

Combine all of the ingredients in a large serving bowl. Toss with the vinaigrette before serving, if using.

Optional dressing not included:

CALORIES: 197 | FAT: 15g | PROTEIN: 11g | TOTAL CARBS: 5.8g | DIETARY FIBER: 2g | NET CARBS: 3.8g

Shaved Brussels Sprouts and Kale Salad

 EGG-FREE makes 8 servings · prep time: 15 minutes (not including time to cook bacon)

This is one of those salads that you would order every single time you visited your favorite restaurant. You might even go to that restaurant specifically to order this salad. The bitterness of the kale and Brussels sprouts combined with the saltiness of the bacon and the creaminess of the blue cheese pair so perfectly with the Citrus Vinaigrette.

ingredients

1 bunch lacinato kale, destemmed and thinly sliced

10 ounces fresh Brussels sprouts, shaved

4 slices bacon, cooked crisp and chopped

½ cup roasted and salted pecan halves

½ cup crumbled blue cheese

Citrus Vinaigrette (page 141), for serving (optional)

directions

Combine all of the ingredients in a large mixing bowl. Toss with the vinaigrette before serving, if using.

tip: Try topping this salad with grilled chicken or salmon to make it a full meal.

Optional dressing not included:

CALORIES: 114 | FAT: 9g | PROTEIN: 5g | TOTAL CARBS: 5.5g | DIETARY FIBER: 2.5g | NET CARBS: 3g

NET CARBS
3g

Greek Salad

  makes 4 servings · prep time: 15 minutes

Ten out of ten times, if I see a Greek salad on a restaurant menu, I will order it. I just love the combination of fresh Mediterranean-inspired ingredients. A couple years ago, I traveled to the beautiful Greek island of Santorini and was surprised to see that a traditional Greek salad does not contain lettuce, and the feta cheese is served in large chunks on top of the salad. It was simply heavenly. Just one bite of this lettuce-based variation whisks me away to the Mediterranean.

ingredients

1 large head romaine lettuce, chopped

1 mini seedless cucumber, halved lengthwise and sliced into half-moons

3 ounces salami, sliced into strips

⅓ cup crumbled feta cheese

⅓ cup halved cherry tomatoes

¼ cup halved and pitted Kalamata olives

A few thin slices red onion

Greek Feta Dressing (page 140), for serving (optional)

directions

Combine all of the ingredients in a large serving bowl. Toss with the dressing before serving, if using.

tip: *This salad is also fantastic with Cucumber Sauce (page 144) as the dressing.*

Optional dressing not included:

CALORIES: 172 | FAT: 12g | PROTEIN: 9g | TOTAL CARBS: 7.5g | DIETARY FIBER: 3.5g | NET CARBS: 4g

Taco Wedge Salad

 EGG-FREE · **NUT-FREE** · makes 4 servings · prep time: 15 minutes (not including time to make taco meat)

Taco salad is one of the meals that I eat the most; I never get tired of it. The great thing about taco salad is that there are no rules. You can use any type of lettuce or cheese you have on hand. You can even make the taco meat with ground turkey or ground chicken. I also love to throw leftover veggies on top.

ingredients

1 head iceberg lettuce, cut into 4 wedges

1 pound cooked taco seasoned ground beef (see tips, page 138)

1 cup shredded sharp cheddar cheese

½ cup sliced black olives

½ cup halved cherry tomatoes

1 medium avocado, peeled, pitted, and sliced

Torn fresh cilantro, for garnish (optional)

Avocado Ranch Dressing (page 142), for serving (optional)

directions

Top each iceberg wedge with one-quarter each of the taco meat, cheese, olives, tomatoes, and avocado slices. Garnish with cilantro, if desired, and serve with the dressing, if using.

tips: For quick-and-easy meal prep, I always prepare salad toppings and keep them in glass containers in the refrigerator, sort of like a mini salad bar.

Also, when I make taco meat, I usually cook 2 to 3 pounds at a time and freeze some for later. These two tips alone save me massive amounts of time in the kitchen.

Optional dressing not included:

CALORIES: 395 | FAT: 27g | PROTEIN: 31g | TOTAL CARBS: 10g | DIETARY FIBER: 4.5g | NET CARBS: 5.5g

Cucumber Dill Tuna Salad

makes 4 servings · prep time: 10 minutes

I always keep a stock of high-quality canned tuna in my pantry, the goal being to have something healthy on hand that is quick to prepare. This tuna salad is perfect for rushed weekday lunches or for when I am nearing the end of my groceries and am down to just pantry staples and condiments. I love to serve it with fresh tomatoes and butter lettuce leaves to make wraps.

ingredients

2 (5-ounce) cans sustainably caught tuna, drained

1 mini seedless cucumber, chopped

1 small dill pickle, chopped

1 tablespoon plus 1 teaspoon chopped fresh dill weed

1 tablespoon chopped fresh chives

½ teaspoon garlic powder

¼ teaspoon sea salt

¼ teaspoon ground black pepper

¼ cup mayonnaise

1½ teaspoons Dijon mustard

directions

Place all of the ingredients in a medium mixing bowl and mix until well incorporated.

CALORIES: 159 | FAT: 11g | PROTEIN: 15g | TOTAL CARBS: 0.5g | DIETARY FIBER: 0g | NET CARBS: 0.5g

Barbecue Chicken Mockaroni Salad

NET CARBS
5g

 NUT-FREE

makes 8 servings · prep time: 15 minutes (not including time to cook chicken or bacon)
cook time: 20 minutes

If you are tired of passing up those giant bowls of macaroni salad at summer cookouts, then this is the recipe for you—the perfect keto potluck dish to take to a party. Bringing this dish gives you the added bonus of knowing for sure that there will be something there you can eat.

ingredients

1 large head cauliflower, cut into bite-sized florets

Sea salt and ground black pepper

8 ounces boneless, skinless chicken breasts or thighs, cooked and chopped

6 slices bacon, cooked crisp and chopped

2 tablespoons dill pickle relish

2 ribs celery, sliced

½ cup diced red bell peppers

½ small red onion, diced (about ¼ cup)

¼ cup full-fat sour cream

¼ cup mayonnaise

¼ cup Barbecue Sauce (page 145)

1 tablespoon prepared yellow mustard

tips: Roasting the cauliflower dry keeps the salad from becoming soupy.

This salad tastes great either warm or cold.

directions

1. Preheat the oven to 425°F. Line a rimmed baking sheet with parchment paper or a silicone baking mat.

2. Spread the cauliflower evenly across the baking sheet and sprinkle generously with salt and pepper. Roast for 20 minutes, or until the cauliflower is tender. Remove from the oven and let cool.

3. While the cauliflower is roasting, place the chicken, bacon, relish, celery, bell peppers, onion, sour cream, mayonnaise, barbecue sauce, and mustard in a large mixing bowl. Mix until the ingredients are well combined.

4. Once the cauliflower has cooled, fold it into the rest of the salad ingredients. Store leftovers in the refrigerator for up to 1 week.

CALORIES: 161 | FAT: 10g | PROTEIN: 12g | TOTAL CARBS: 8g | DIETARY FIBER: 3g | NET CARBS: 5g | ERYTHRITOL: 1g

Breakfast

Fortune Cookie Waffles / 60

Ham and Spinach
Eggs Benedict / 62

Cheesy Pico Eggs / 64

Sausage Balls / 66

Sour Cream and Chive
Egg Clouds / 68

Ham and Cheese Waffles / 70

Chicken Cordon Bleu Frittata / 72

Fortune Cookie Waffles

NUT-FREE

makes 4 large Belgian-style waffles (½ waffle per serving)
prep time: 10 minutes · cook time: 20 minutes

These waffles taste like breakfast and dessert all in one. When I made them the first time, the flavor instantly reminded me of fortune cookies, hence the name. They have just enough sweetness to be delicious on their own but are equally delicious topped with a little bit of sugar-free maple syrup, as shown. Although these waffles don't come with a fortune inside, they will definitely leave you feeling satisfied.

ingredients

4 ounces full-fat cream cheese (½ cup), softened

4 large eggs

2 tablespoons granular erythritol

2 tablespoons heavy cream

2 teaspoons pure vanilla extract

⅓ cup coconut flour

2 teaspoons baking powder

Butter or ghee, for the waffle iron

directions

1. Place the cream cheese, eggs, erythritol, heavy cream, and vanilla extract in a blender. Pulse until the mixture is smooth and the ingredients are well combined.

2. Add the coconut flour and baking powder and pulse to combine. It may be necessary to use a rubber spatula to scrape down the blender jar and mix in any coconut flour that sticks to the sides.

3. Lightly grease the waffle iron with butter. Ladle the batter into the center of the waffle iron; the amount will vary depending on the capacity of your waffle iron. Consult the manufacturer's directions for the recommended amount of batter.

4. Cook for 5 minutes, or until the waffle iron stops steaming. Repeat this process with the remaining batter, regreasing the waffle iron between waffles.

time-saving tip:

Make a double or triple batch of these waffles and freeze them for later! I recommend reheating them in a toaster or toaster oven.

CALORIES: 119 | FAT: 9g | PROTEIN: 5g | TOTAL CARBS: 3.5g | DIETARY FIBER: 1.6g | NET CARBS: 1.9g | ERYTHRITOL: 3.8g

Ham and Spinach Eggs Benedict

 NUT-FREE

makes 4 servings · prep time: 15 minutes · cook time: 25 minutes

Eggs Benedict is and always has been one of my all-time favorite breakfast dishes. A perfectly poached egg is nothing short of amazing. That delicious, creamy yolk mixing with the rich flavors of hollandaise and Canadian bacon is a match made in heaven.

ingredients

2 tablespoons olive oil

8 packed cups fresh spinach leaves

4 ounces cremini mushrooms, thinly sliced

2 cloves garlic, minced

1 teaspoon sea salt

½ teaspoon ground black pepper

8 large eggs

¼ teaspoon white vinegar

For serving:

1 tomato, cut into 8 slices

8 ounces Canadian bacon or thinly sliced ham, warmed

¾ cup Easy Peasy Blender Hollandaise (page 146), warm

⅓ cup crumbled feta cheese

2 tablespoons chopped fresh chives

directions

1. Heat the olive oil in a large skillet over medium heat. Add the spinach, mushrooms, garlic, salt, and pepper and sauté until the spinach is wilted and the mushrooms have released their liquid, about 8 minutes. Reduce the heat to low to keep the mixture warm.

2. Crack an egg into a small ramekin.

3. Bring a small pot of water to a rapid boil. Add the vinegar to the water and, using a spoon, give the water a swirl to create a whirlpool effect in the center of the pot. Gently slide the egg into the center of the whirlpool. After 2 minutes, use a slotted spoon to remove the egg from the water. Repeat this process with the remaining eggs.

4. To serve, divide the spinach and mushroom mixture evenly among 4 plates. Top each plate with 2 tomato slices, 2 slices of Canadian bacon, and 2 poached eggs and then one-quarter each of the hollandaise, feta cheese, and chives.

time-saving tip:

The spinach and mushroom base for this recipe also makes an amazing dinner side dish. Make a double batch of it for dinner and then half of the work for breakfast is already done!

CALORIES: 541 | FAT: 42g | PROTEIN: 33g | TOTAL CARBS: 9.5g | DIETARY FIBER: 3g | NET CARBS: 6.5g

Cheesy Pico Eggs

NET CARBS
3.5g

 makes 1 serving · prep time: 5 minutes · cook time: 5 minutes

If you don't already add heavy cream to scrambled eggs, then this recipe just might change the way you make eggs forever. It is amazing how just a touch of cream can completely transform the texture of eggs, making them so light and fluffy. Feel free to use any cheese you have on hand. Another one of my favorites for this dish is pepper Jack. It pairs so well with pico de gallo. Serve these eggs with your favorite breakfast meat and some fresh avocado and you've got yourself a meal!

ingredients

3 large eggs

1 tablespoon heavy cream

¼ teaspoon sea salt

Pinch of ground black pepper

1 tablespoon butter or olive oil

2 tablespoons shredded mozzarella cheese

2 tablespoons Pico de Gallo (page 41)

tip: These eggs are also great topped with Roasted Tomatillo Salsa Verde (page 139).

directions

1. Crack the eggs into a small bowl and whisk with a fork. Add the heavy cream, salt, and pepper and whisk until the ingredients are well incorporated.

2. Heat the butter in a large skillet over medium heat. When the pan is hot, add the eggs and, using a heatproof rubber spatula, gently stir and start to fold the eggs. Let them begin to set, then fold them once more. Repeat this process until the eggs are cooked to your desired level of doneness. Scrambling them slowly and not overworking them will produce amazingly fluffy eggs.

3. Top the eggs with the mozzarella and pico de gallo before serving.

CALORIES: 415 | FAT: 35g | PROTEIN: 24g | TOTAL CARBS: 3.7g | DIETARY FIBER: 0.2g | NET CARBS: 3.5g

Sausage Balls

makes 24 balls (4 per serving) · prep time: 10 minutes · cook time: 20 minutes

This is one of my favorite recipes in this book. These sausage balls are so simple to make, and they are perfect for any meal. I always keep a batch in the refrigerator for those days when I just don't feel like cooking. I like to make a double or triple batch, portion them out, and freeze them for later. Cook once, eat multiple times! I like to serve these with Barbecue Sauce (page 145) and Avocado Ranch Dressing (page 142) for dipping.

ingredients

1 pound bulk Italian sausage

1 cup blanched almond flour

1 cup shredded sharp cheddar cheese

¼ cup grated Parmesan cheese

1 large egg

1 tablespoon dried minced onions

2 teaspoons baking powder

directions

1. Preheat the oven to 350°F. Set a a wire cooling rack inside a rimmed baking sheet.

2. Place all of the ingredients in a large mixing bowl and, using your hands, mix until well incorporated.

3. Form the meat mixture into 1½- to 2-inch meatballs, making a total of 24.

4. Place the meatballs on the wire rack. Bake for 20 minutes, or until golden brown.

CALORIES: 374 | FAT: 31g | PROTEIN: 22g | TOTAL CARBS: 5.5g | DIETARY FIBER: 2g | NET CARBS: 3.5g

Sour Cream and Chive Egg Clouds

 NUT-FREE

makes 8 egg clouds (2 per serving) · prep time: 10 minutes
cook time: 6 minutes

 NET CARBS
2.3g

These egg clouds are one of my favorite ways to jazz up my morning breakfast routine and get new flavors and textures from my eggs. They are also a great way to get kids excited about eating eggs for breakfast.

ingredients

8 large eggs

¼ cup shredded sharp white cheddar cheese

¼ cup full-fat sour cream

1 teaspoon garlic powder

2 fresh chives, sliced, divided

2 teaspoons salted butter

tip: *Try mixing things up a bit and adding some chopped bacon or crumbled sausage to the egg white mixture.*

directions

1. Preheat the oven to 450°F. Line a rimmed baking sheet with parchment paper or a silicone baking mat.

2. Separate the eggs, pouring the whites into a large mixing bowl and each yolk into a small ramekin or bowl.

3. Using an electric hand mixer or a stand mixer, whip the egg whites until they are fluffy and stiff peaks start to form.

4. Using a rubber spatula, gently fold the cheese, sour cream, garlic powder, and half of the chives into the whipped egg whites.

5. Spoon the mixture into 8 separate mounds on the prepared baking sheet. Use a large spoon to make a well in the center of each cloud. Gently pour an egg yolk into each well.

6. Bake for 6 minutes, or until the egg clouds are golden brown on top and the yolks are set.

7. Place ¼ teaspoon of butter on top of each yolk, then garnish with the remaining chives.

CALORIES: 214 | FAT: 16g | PROTEIN: 15g | TOTAL CARBS: 2.3g | DIETARY FIBER: 0g | NET CARBS: 2.3g

Ham and Cheese Waffles

 makes 8 waffles (1 per serving) · prep time: 10 minutes · cook time: 40 minutes

These savory ham and cheese waffles are delicious with a fried egg on top, or you can cut them into dipper sticks and serve them with sugar-free maple syrup. Better yet, try them with an egg and syrup. The combination of sweet and savory is everything a great breakfast should be.

ingredients

½ cup coconut flour

2 tablespoons granular erythritol

1 teaspoon ground cinnamon

½ teaspoon baking powder

½ teaspoon sea salt

5 large eggs

½ cup heavy cream

½ cup water

¼ cup (½ stick) butter, melted (but not hot)

1 teaspoon pure vanilla extract

1 cup chopped ham

1 cup shredded sharp cheddar cheese

Butter or coconut oil, for the waffle iron

tip: These waffles freeze and reheat very well, making them a perfect option for quick-and-easy meal prep. I recommend reheating them in the toaster or toaster oven.

directions

1. Place the coconut flour, erythritol, cinnamon, baking powder, and salt in a large mixing bowl. Using a whisk, mix until the ingredients are well combined.

2. Crack the eggs into a separate mixing bowl. Add the heavy cream, water, melted butter, and vanilla extract and whisk to combine.

3. Slowly pour the egg mixture into the dry ingredients, whisking as you pour. Mix until the ingredients are well incorporated.

4. Using a rubber spatula, fold the ham and cheese into the batter.

5. Lightly grease a waffle iron with butter. Ladle the batter into the center of the waffle iron; the amount will vary depending on the capacity of your waffle iron. Consult the manufacturer's directions for the recommended amount of batter.

6. Cook for 5 minutes, or until the waffle iron stops steaming. Repeat this process with the remaining batter, regreasing the waffle iron between waffles.

CALORIES: 211 | FAT: 16g | PROTEIN: 10g | TOTAL CARBS: 5.6g | DIETARY FIBER: 2.6g | NET CARBS: 3g | ERYTHRITOL: 3.8g

Chicken Cordon Bleu Frittata

 NUT-FREE · makes 6 servings · prep time: 10 minutes · cook time: 30 minutes

All the delicious flavors of a classic dinner recipe, but in breakfast form. This is one of my favorite recipes for repurposing leftovers, especially around the holidays. Have leftover Thanksgiving turkey or Christmas ham? This is a great way to repurpose dinner into a delicious breakfast that the whole family will love.

ingredients

10 large eggs

¼ cup heavy cream

2 cloves garlic, minced

½ teaspoon sea salt

¼ teaspoon ground black pepper

6 ounces Swiss cheese, cut into 8 slices, divided

8 ounces chicken breast, cooked and chopped, divided

8 ounces ham, chopped, divided

For serving (optional):

¼ cup baby arugula

¼ cup cherry tomatoes, halved

1 chive, chopped

directions

1. Crack the eggs into a large mixing bowl and whisk. Add the heavy cream, garlic, salt, and pepper and whisk until well combined.

2. Chop 4 slices of the Swiss cheese and add it to the egg mixture. Mix in half of the chicken and half of the ham.

3. Preheat the oven to 375°F.

4. Heat a large ovenproof skillet over medium heat. Pour the egg mixture into the skillet and cook until the bottom and sides begin to set, about 10 minutes.

5. Top with the remaining cheese slices, chicken, and ham. Transfer the skillet to the oven and bake for 20 minutes, or until the center is set.

6. Before serving, top with the arugula, tomatoes, and chive, if desired.

time-saving tip: Using rotisserie chicken for this recipe is a great way to cut down on time spent in the kitchen. Batch cooking chicken breasts and freezing them in individual portions is another great way to make mealtime a breeze.

CALORIES: 353 | FAT: 22g | PROTEIN: 35g | TOTAL CARBS: 2.8g | DIETARY FIBER: 0g | NET CARBS: 2.8g

LUNCH
AND
Dinner

Pork Chops with Herbed
Goat Cheese Butter / 76

Spicy Sausage and Cabbage
Stir-Fry / 78

Zucchini Noodles with
Hamburger Gravy / 80

Chicken Sausage and
Vegetable Skillet / 82

Sloppy Joe–Stuffed Peppers / 84

Cheesy Salsa Verde
Chicken Casserole / 86

Greek Meatballs / 88

Grilled New York Strip Steak with
Blue Cheese Dijon Cream Sauce / 90

Fish Taco Bowls / 92

Herbed Chicken with
Mushrooms / 94

Skillet Chicken Parmesan / 96

Shrimp Piccata / 98

Salisbury Steak / 100

Buffalo Chicken Roasted
Cabbage Steaks / 102

Zucchini Noodles with
Pesto Cream Sauce / 104

Pork Chops with Herbed Goat Cheese Butter

 EGG-FREE   NUT-FREE   makes 4 servings · prep time: 10 minutes · cook time: 12 minutes

The herbed goat cheese butter in this recipe elevates already tender and juicy pork chops to a whole new level. If you happen to have any leftover butter, it is amazing smeared on Buttery Garlic Crescent Rolls (page 38) or on top of chicken. I love to serve these pork chops with Sautéed Green Beans with Ham (page 118).

ingredients

2 tablespoons olive oil

4 thick-cut boneless pork loin chops (about 2 pounds)

Sea salt and ground black pepper

For the herbed goat cheese butter:

¼ cup (½ stick) salted butter, **softened**

¼ cup fresh (soft) goat cheese

½ teaspoon chopped fresh chives

½ teaspoon chopped fresh flat-leaf parsley

½ teaspoon chopped fresh rosemary

¼ teaspoon chopped fresh thyme

¼ teaspoon garlic powder

directions

1. Heat the olive oil in a large skillet over medium heat. Season the pork chops generously on both sides with salt and pepper.

2. Place the pork chops in the skillet and sear on both sides until they are golden brown and cooked all the way through, about 6 minutes per side.

3. While the pork chops are cooking, make the herbed goat cheese butter: Place the butter, goat cheese, chives, parsley, rosemary, thyme, and garlic powder in a small bowl. Mix until the ingredients are well incorporated.

4. Top each pork chop with one-quarter of the herbed goat cheese butter before serving.

CALORIES: 507 | FAT: 32g | PROTEIN: 48g | TOTAL CARBS: 0.5g | DIETARY FIBER: 0g | NET CARBS: 0.5g

Spicy Sausage and Cabbage Stir-Fry

makes 6 servings · prep time: 15 minutes · cook time: 15 minutes

ingredients

1 tablespoon olive oil

1 pound bulk hot Italian sausage

4 cloves garlic, minced

1½ teaspoons grated gingerroot

½ teaspoon sea salt

¼ teaspoon ground black pepper

4 ounces cremini mushrooms, thinly sliced

1 head napa cabbage, thinly shredded

1 small green bell pepper, julienned

1 small red bell pepper, julienned

2 tablespoons unseasoned rice vinegar

2 tablespoons coconut aminos or gluten-free soy sauce

2 teaspoons toasted sesame oil

2 tablespoons chopped fresh chives, for garnish

2 tablespoons toasted sesame seeds, for garnish

directions

1. Heat the olive oil in a large skillet over medium-high heat. When the pan is hot, add the sausage, garlic, ginger, salt, and pepper. Using a heatproof spatula, break up the meat and cook until browned, about 5 minutes.

2. Use a slotted spoon to remove the sausage from the skillet, leaving the drippings in the pan.

3. To the same skillet, add the mushrooms. Once they are tender and have released their liquid, add the cabbage. Cook for 3 to 4 minutes, until the cabbage just starts to wilt.

4. Add the bell peppers, vinegar, coconut aminos, and sesame oil. Cook until the peppers are crisp-tender, about 3 minutes.

5. Return the sausage to the pan and mix in. Garnish with the chives and sesame seeds before serving.

CALORIES: 275 | FAT: 20g | PROTEIN: 14g | TOTAL CARBS: 9g | DIETARY FIBER: 3g | NET CARBS: 6g

Zucchini Noodles with Hamburger Gravy

makes 6 servings · prep time: 10 minutes (plus time to salt zucchini)
cook time: 30 minutes

Reminiscent of late-night diner food from your local greasy spoon, this hamburger gravy just screams comfort food to me. Besides being great over noodles, this gravy is also amazing on top of Cheddar Jalapeño Bacon Biscuits (page 42). Top it with a perfectly yolky fried egg and you have repurposed dinner leftovers into a mouthwatering breakfast dish.

ingredients

4 large zucchini, spiral-sliced

3½ teaspoons sea salt, divided

2 tablespoons butter

1 small onion, diced (about ½ cup)

4 cloves garlic, minced

½ teaspoon dried rubbed sage

¼ teaspoon ground black pepper

1 pound ground beef

1½ cups heavy cream

½ cup grated Parmesan cheese, plus extra for garnish

3 tablespoons chopped fresh flat-leaf parsley, for garnish

time-saving tip: Buy zucchini in bulk when you see it on sale, spiral-slice it into noodles and portion them out, then freeze them until you are ready to use them. Salt and rest after thawing.

directions

1. Lay the zucchini noodles in a single layer on a bed of paper towels. Sprinkle them with 2½ teaspoons of the salt and let rest for 10 to 15 minutes. The salt will help draw out the excess moisture so that the zucchini noodles do not water down the gravy. When the noodles have released their liquid, place a layer of fresh paper towels on top and dab away the excess moisture, then set the noodles aside.

2. While the noodles are resting, make the gravy: Heat the butter in a large skillet over medium heat. When the pan is hot, add the onion, garlic, remaining teaspoon of salt, sage, and pepper. Cook until the onion is translucent and the garlic is fragrant.

3. Add the ground beef to the skillet, breaking it up with a heatproof spatula, and cook until browned, 5 to 7 minutes.

4. Mix in the heavy cream and Parmesan, reduce the heat to low, and simmer until thickened, about 10 minutes.

5. Add the zucchini noodles to the pan, toss them in the gravy, and cook for 2 to 3 minutes, until the noodles are tender but not mushy.

6. Garnish with the parsley and some extra Parmesan before serving.

CALORIES: 293 | FAT: 22g | PROTEIN: 13g | TOTAL CARBS: 8.5g | DIETARY FIBER: 2.4g | NET CARBS: 6.1g

Chicken Sausage and Vegetable Skillet

makes 6 servings · prep time: 15 minutes · cook time: 25 minutes

I love how simple this dish is to make and how clean yet satisfying the ingredients are. The great thing about this recipe is that you can use any meat and veggies you have on hand. There is also the added bonus of dirtying only one pan. Healthy, satisfying, *and* only one pan? I'll take it!

ingredients

3 tablespoons olive oil

5 chicken sausage links, sliced

2 cloves garlic, minced

1 small red onion, cut into large chunks

1 small zucchini (about 6 inches), halved lengthwise and sliced into half-moons

1 small yellow squash, halved lengthwise and sliced into half-moons

1 small red bell pepper, cut into large chunks

1 small yellow bell pepper, cut into large chunks

6 cremini mushrooms, quartered

½ teaspoon Italian seasoning

½ teaspoon red pepper flakes

Sea salt and ground black pepper (optional)

directions

1. Heat the olive oil in a large skillet over medium heat. Add the sausage, garlic, and onion and sauté until the sausage is browned and the onion is translucent, about 10 minutes.

2. Add the zucchini, yellow squash, bell peppers, mushrooms, Italian seasoning, and red pepper flakes to the skillet and sauté for an additional 10 to 15 minutes, until the vegetables are crisp-tender.

3. Taste and add salt and pepper, if desired.

CALORIES: 205 | FAT: 14g | PROTEIN: 14g | TOTAL CARBS: 5.6g | DIETARY FIBER: 1.6g | NET CARBS: 4g

Sloppy Joe-Stuffed Peppers

makes 8 servings · prep time: 10 minutes · cook time: 25 minutes

Growing up, we ate a lot of sloppy Joes—that notorious cloyingly sweet canned sauce cooked with ground beef and served on a big hamburger bun. It was usually accompanied by tater tots and ketchup, and I loved every last bite. But as I grew up and my palate began to mature and change, my childhood favorite became less appealing to me. It wasn't until I made my own version from scratch with real-food ingredients that I began to love the sloppy meat mixture once again.

ingredients

4 large bell peppers (any color)

2 tablespoons olive oil

1 small onion, chopped (about ½ cup)

1 rib celery, chopped

3 cloves garlic, minced

1½ pounds ground beef

1 cup tomato sauce or crushed tomatoes

¼ cup reduced-sugar ketchup

1 tablespoon Worcestershire sauce

1 tablespoon Dijon mustard

2 teaspoons chili powder

1 teaspoon ground cumin

¾ teaspoon sea salt

2 tablespoons chopped fresh flat-leaf parsley

directions

1. Preheat the oven to 375°F. Line a rimmed baking sheet with parchment paper or a silicone baking mat.

2. Cut the peppers in half vertically and remove the ribs and seeds. Place the peppers cut side up on the prepared baking sheet and bake for 20 to 25 minutes, until they are tender.

3. While the peppers are in the oven, make the sloppy Joe mixture: Heat the olive oil in a large skillet over medium heat. When the pan is hot, add the onion, celery, and garlic. Cook until the onion and celery are soft and the garlic is fragrant.

4. Add the ground beef, breaking it up with a heatproof spatula, and cook until browned, about 8 minutes.

5. Mix in the tomato sauce, ketchup, Worcestershire sauce, Dijon mustard, chili powder, cumin, and salt. Simmer for 5 to 7 minutes, until the sauce has thickened.

6. Stuff the sloppy Joe mixture into the pepper halves and garnish with the parsley.

CALORIES: 205 | FAT: 10g | PROTEIN: 19g | TOTAL CARBS: 8.5g | DIETARY FIBER: 2.5g | NET CARBS: 6g

Cheesy Salsa Verde Chicken Casserole

NET CARBS
4g

 makes 8 servings · prep time: 10 minutes · cook time: 25 minutes

I am a huge fan of all things Mexican inspired. It is always Taco Tuesday in my heart. This casserole comes kid and husband approved. They gobbled it down faster than the mere 25 minutes it took me to bake it. It has been in steady rotation in my home ever since.

ingredients

2 pounds boneless, skinless chicken breasts or thighs, cut into bite-sized pieces

1½ cups shredded mozzarella cheese, divided

1½ cups shredded sharp cheddar cheese, divided

1¼ cups salsa verde, store-bought or homemade (page 139), divided

¾ cup full-fat sour cream

1½ teaspoons sea salt

1 teaspoon chili powder

1 teaspoon ground cumin

¼ teaspoon ground black pepper

1 medium avocado, peeled, pitted, and diced

For garnish (optional):

¼ cup Pico de Gallo (page 41)

Torn fresh cilantro

directions

1. Place the chicken, ¾ cup of the mozzarella, ¾ cup of the cheddar cheese, ¾ cup of the salsa verde, sour cream, salt, chili powder, cumin, and pepper in a large mixing bowl. Mix until the ingredients are well incorporated.

2. Preheat the oven to 400°F.

3. Pour ¼ cup of the salsa verde into a 2-quart casserole dish. Pour the chicken mixture on top and spread it out in an even layer. Top with the remaining salsa verde, mozzarella, and cheddar cheese.

4. Bake for 25 minutes, or until the casserole is bubbling.

5. Top with the diced avocado and garnish with the pico de gallo and cilantro, if desired.

tip: I love to serve this casserole with Green Onion and Lime Cauliflower Rice (page 110).

CALORIES: 383 | FAT: 26g | PROTEIN: 32g | TOTAL CARBS: 5.4g | DIETARY FIBER: 1.4g | NET CARBS: 4g

Greek Meatballs

 NUT-FREE

**makes 36 meatballs (6 per serving) · prep time: 15 minutes
cook time: 15 minutes**

NET CARBS
2g

This is hands down my favorite recipe in this book. The cool cucumber sauce pairs perfectly with the savory meatballs. My Green Onion and Lime Cauliflower Rice (page 110) complements this dish perfectly—it was like they were made to go together. This is also one of my favorite recipes for meal prep. The meatballs freeze well, and the cucumber sauce can be whipped up in no time flat.

ingredients

2 pounds ground beef (see tip)

1 small onion

½ cup crumbled feta cheese

2 cloves garlic, minced

1 large egg

2 tablespoons chopped fresh
flat-leaf parsley

1 tablespoon chopped fresh
mint

1 teaspoon dried oregano leaves

1 teaspoon sea salt

¼ teaspoon ground black
pepper

2 tablespoons olive oil

Cucumber Sauce (page 144),
for serving (optional)

A few sprigs fresh mint, for
garnish

directions

1. Put the ground beef in a large mixing bowl. Using a Microplane, grate the onion into the bowl.

2. Add the feta, garlic, egg, parsley, mint, oregano, salt, and pepper. Using your hands, mix until the ingredients are well incorporated. Form the mixture into 36 meatballs, about 1½ inches in diameter.

3. Preheat the oven to 350°F.

4. Heat the olive oil in a large ovenproof skillet over medium-high heat. Place the meatballs in the pan and cook until they are browned all over, about 5 minutes.

5. Transfer the skillet to the oven and bake for 10 minutes, or until the meatballs are cooked through. Serve the meatballs with the sauce, garnished with fresh mint sprigs.

tip: These meatballs are also good when made with ground pork, lamb, or any combination of the three meats.

CALORIES: 359 | FAT: 23g | PROTEIN: 34g | TOTAL CARBS: 2.3g | DIETARY FIBER: 0.3g | NET CARBS: 2g

Grilled New York Strip Steak with Blue Cheese Dijon Cream Sauce

 EGG-FREE · NUT-FREE · makes 4 servings · prep time: 10 minutes · cook time: 15 minutes

Why pay high-end steakhouse prices when you can make a perfectly cooked, delicious steak in the comfort of your own home? The cream sauce in this recipe is also delicious on top of broccoli or Brussels sprouts.

ingredients

4 (8-ounce) New York strip steaks, or boneless steaks of choice (see tip)

2 tablespoons olive oil

Sea salt and ground black pepper

For the cream sauce:

1 cup heavy cream

⅓ cup Dijon mustard

¼ cup crumbled blue cheese

3 cloves garlic, minced

2 teaspoons dried minced onions

For garnish:

¼ cup crumbled blue cheese

1 teaspoon chopped fresh chives

directions

1. Drizzle the steaks on both sides with the olive oil and season generously with salt and pepper.

2. Make the cream sauce: In a saucepan over medium heat, combine the heavy cream, Dijon mustard, blue cheese, garlic, and dried onions. Cook until the cheese has melted and the sauce has started to thicken, then reduce the heat to low.

3. Heat a grill pan or large skillet over medium-high heat. When the pan is hot, sear the steaks for 4 to 6 minutes on each side for medium-rare, or until the desired level of doneness is reached.

4. Top each steak with one-quarter of the cream sauce and garnish with one-quarter each of the blue cheese and chives before serving.

tip: For best results, let the steaks come to room temperature before cooking.

CALORIES: 860 | FAT: 71g | PROTEIN: 54g | TOTAL CARBS: 4g | DIETARY FIBER: 0g | NET CARBS: 4g

Fish Taco Bowls

 makes 4 servings · prep time: 15 minutes · cook time: 6 minutes

This recipe is my own personal version of "Taste the Rainbow." You eat with your eyes first, and beautiful food is simply more tantalizing to the taste buds. This is one of my favorite dishes to eat during the hot summer months when heavier foods just don't sound good. I love to serve it with a side of Avocado Ranch Dressing (page 142) or Cucumber Sauce (page 144).

ingredients

1½ pounds wild-caught cod or halibut fillets

3 tablespoons olive oil

2 tablespoons Taco Seasoning (page 138)

2 cups Green Onion and Lime Cauliflower Rice (page 110), warm

1 yellow bell pepper, julienned

1 jalapeño pepper, sliced (optional)

1 avocado, peeled, pitted, and sliced

1 cup cherry tomatoes, halved

1 cup shredded red cabbage

¼ cup sliced black olives

Sea salt and ground black pepper (optional)

Torn fresh cilantro, for garnish (optional)

Lime wedges, for serving

directions

1. Cut the fish into 4 equal-sized pieces. Place the fish, olive oil, and taco seasoning in a large mixing bowl and toss gently to coat. Set aside to marinate while you prepare the taco bowls.

2. Put ½ cup of the cauliflower rice in each of 4 serving bowls. Arrange one-quarter each of the bell pepper, jalapeño, avocado, tomatoes, cabbage, and olives around the outside of each bowl, leaving a space for the fish in the center.

3. Heat a grill pan or large skillet over medium heat. When the pan is hot, add the fish and cook until it is browned and flakes easily, about 3 minutes per side. Taste a small piece of the fish and season with salt and pepper, if desired.

4. Place a piece of fish in the center of each of the arranged bowls. Garnish with cilantro, if desired, and serve each bowl with a lime wedge.

tip: *To make this dish dairy-free and Paleo compliant, use olive oil instead of butter when making the cauliflower rice.*

CALORIES: 370 | FAT: 21g | PROTEIN: 36g | TOTAL CARBS: 13g | DIETARY FIBER: 6g | NET CARBS: 7g

NET CARBS
2.5g

Herbed Chicken with Mushrooms

makes 4 servings · prep time: 10 minutes · cook time: 30 minutes

This chicken and mushroom dish is so tender and juicy and packs so much flavor that it's hard to believe it can be ready and on the table so fast. You've got to love any recipe that calls for inexpensive ingredients, dirties only one pot, and is quick and easy to prepare while still being incredibly flavorful.

ingredients

8 bone-in, skin-on chicken thighs (about 2 pounds)

2 teaspoons sea salt

½ teaspoon ground black pepper

4 teaspoons dried oregano leaves, divided

4 teaspoons dried rosemary leaves, divided

4 teaspoons dried thyme leaves, divided

2 tablespoons olive oil

8 ounces cremini mushrooms, quartered

1 cup chicken stock

2 tablespoons Dijon mustard

2 cloves garlic, minced

Torn fresh flat-leaf parsley, for garnish (optional)

directions

1. Preheat the oven to 400°F.

2. Season the chicken thighs on both sides with the salt, pepper, and 2 teaspoons each of the oregano, rosemary, and thyme.

3. Heat the olive oil in a large cast-iron or other ovenproof skillet over medium heat. When the pan is hot, add the chicken thighs, skin side down. Cook for 5 to 6 minutes, until the skin is nice and crispy.

4. Flip the chicken thighs over and transfer the skillet to the oven. Bake for 15 to 20 minutes, until the chicken is cooked all the way through.

5. Return the skillet to the stovetop. Remove the chicken to a plate and cover to keep warm.

6. Put the mushrooms in the skillet and cook over medium heat for 5 minutes, or until they have released their liquid and are tender.

7. Add the chicken stock, Dijon mustard, garlic, and remaining dried herbs and cook for an additional 3 minutes, until the stock is slightly reduced.

8. Plate the chicken and pour the sauce over the top. Garnish with fresh parsley, if desired.

CALORIES: 392 | FAT: 30g | PROTEIN: 30g | TOTAL CARBS: 4.3g | DIETARY FIBER: 1.8g | NET CARBS: 2.5g

Skillet Chicken Parmesan

NET CARBS
3.3g

 EGG-FREE · NUT-FREE makes 4 servings · prep time: 10 minutes · cook time: 30 minutes

This chicken Parmesan is so good that you won't even miss the traditional breading. This is also a great dish for meal prep because it reheats incredibly well. I recommend reheating it in the oven at 275°F until it is warmed through.

ingredients

1½ pounds boneless, skinless chicken breasts

Sea salt and ground black pepper

2 tablespoons olive oil

1 cup marinara sauce

1 cup shredded mozzarella cheese

1 teaspoon Italian seasoning

¼ cup shredded Parmesan cheese

Fresh basil, for garnish

directions

1. Preheat the oven to 350°F.

2. Season the chicken generously on both sides with salt and pepper.

3. Heat the olive oil in a large cast-iron or other ovenproof skillet over medium-high heat. When the pan is hot, add the chicken and sear until it is golden brown on one side.

4. Flip the chicken over and top with the marinara, mozzarella cheese, and Italian seasoning. Transfer the skillet to the oven and bake for 20 minutes, or until the chicken is cooked all the way through.

5. Top the chicken with the Parmesan cheese and return the skillet to the oven for 5 more minutes.

6. Garnish with fresh basil before serving.

tip: Be sure to look for a marinara sauce made with clean ingredients—only vegetables and spices. Alternatively, you can visit my site, peaceloveandlowcarb. com, for a few low-carb marinara sauce variations.

CALORIES: 451 | FAT: 16g | PROTEIN: 55g | TOTAL CARBS: 3.8g | DIETARY FIBER: 0.5g | NET CARBS: 3.3g

Shrimp Piccata

 makes 4 servings · prep time: 15 minutes · cook time: 8 minutes

I'm sure you have probably already tried chicken piccata, and maybe even pork piccata, but have you made it with shrimp? If not, then you are in for a real treat. This shrimp piccata is so fresh and light. I like to serve it with Green Onion and Lime Cauliflower Rice (page 110) and some fresh greens.

ingredients

1 pound extra-large shrimp (26/30)

Sea salt and ground black pepper

3 tablespoons butter

3 cloves garlic, minced

⅓ cup chicken stock

3 tablespoons capers

1 tablespoon chopped fresh flat-leaf parsley

1 tablespoon fresh lemon juice

1 teaspoon grated lemon zest

Lemon slices, for serving (optional)

directions

1. Peel and devein the shrimp, then rinse and pat them dry. Season the shrimp generously with salt and pepper and set aside.

2. Heat the butter in a large skillet over medium heat. When the pan is hot, add the garlic and sauté until fragrant, about 2 minutes.

3. Add the shrimp to the pan and cook until they start to turn pink and are almost cooked through. You don't want them to be completely cooked at this stage, as you will add them back to the pan later. Using a slotted spoon, remove the shrimp from the pan and set aside.

4. Add the chicken stock and use a heatproof spatula to deglaze the pan, scraping up and mixing in any bits stuck to the pan. Add the capers, parsley, lemon juice, and lemon zest and stir to combine.

5. Return the shrimp to the skillet and cook until they have finished cooking all the way through. Serve with lemon slices, if desired.

CALORIES: 182 | FAT: 10g | PROTEIN: 20g | TOTAL CARBS: 2.5g | DIETARY FIBER: 0.3g | NET CARBS: 2.2g

Salisbury Steak

NET CARBS
6.2g

makes 4 servings · prep time: 15 minutes · cook time: 25 minutes

When I think about Salisbury steak, the first thing that comes to mind is the TV dinners from the eighties that came in aluminum trays and included Salisbury steak, instant mashed potatoes, corn, and cinnamon-and-sugar baked apples. I promise you that this recipe is a lot more satisfying—and a lot healthier, too. Time and time again, I have found that the key to sustainability in a low-carb, keto lifestyle doesn't lie in the things you give up, but in the creativity you use to rework things. I am all about re-creating classic comfort food into healthy, real-food versions.

ingredients

For the patties:

1½ pounds ground beef

1 large egg

2 cloves garlic, minced

1 small onion, diced (about ½ cup)

3 tablespoons reduced-sugar ketchup

1 tablespoon plus 1 teaspoon Dijon mustard

2 teaspoons beef bouillon granules, or 2 beef bouillon cubes, crushed

2 teaspoons Worcestershire sauce

1 tablespoon olive oil

For the sauce:

2 cloves garlic, minced

1 small onion, diced (about ½ cup)

2 cups beef stock

2 tablespoons coconut flour

1 tablespoon Dijon mustard

½ teaspoon sea salt

¼ teaspoon ground black pepper

8 ounces cremini mushrooms, thinly sliced

2 tablespoons chopped fresh flat-leaf parsley, plus extra for garnish (optional)

directions

1. Make the patties: Place the ground beef, egg, garlic, onion, ketchup, Dijon mustard, beef bouillon, and Worcestershire sauce in a large mixing bowl. Mix with your hands until the ingredients are well incorporated. Form the mixture into 6 equal-sized oval patties.

2. Heat the olive oil in a large skillet over medium-high heat. Add the patties and cook until they are browned on both sides, about 3 minutes per side. Remove the patties to a plate, leaving the drippings in the pan, and cover the patties to keep warm.

3. Make the sauce: Reduce the heat under the skillet to medium, put the garlic and onion in the skillet, and cook until the garlic is fragrant and the onion is translucent, about 5 minutes.

CALORIES: 357 | FAT: 17g | PROTEIN: 39g | TOTAL CARBS: 8.5g | DIETARY FIBER: 2.3g | NET CARBS: 6.2g

4. Add the beef stock and use a heatproof spatula to deglaze the pan, scraping up and mixing in any bits stuck to the pan.

5. Whisking continuously, mix in the coconut flour, Dijon mustard, salt, and pepper. Add the mushrooms and parsley and simmer for 5 minutes, stirring occasionally.

6. Reduce the heat to low and return the patties to the pan. Cook for 5 to 7 minutes, until the patties are hot and the sauce has thickened. Garnish with additional parsley, if desired, before serving.

Buffalo Chicken
Roasted Cabbage Steaks

 makes 6 servings · prep time: 15 minutes · cook time: 30 minutes

I love to serve these cabbage steaks during football season when we have a house full of people cheering on the Seahawks. It is always a quick-and-easy crowd-pleaser.

ingredients

1 large head green cabbage

2 tablespoons olive oil

Sea salt and ground black pepper

2 tablespoons butter

1 cup Buffalo wing sauce

3 cups shredded rotisserie chicken

½ cup crumbled blue cheese

2 ribs celery, sliced

2 green onions, sliced, for garnish (optional)

directions

1. Preheat the oven to 425°F. Line a rimmed baking sheet with parchment paper or a silicone baking mat.

2. Slice the head of cabbage into 6 equal slices, cutting from the top down through the core. Arrange the cabbage slices in a single layer on the prepared baking sheet.

3. Drizzle the cabbage with the olive oil and season generously with salt and pepper. Roast for 30 minutes, flipping the slices over halfway through.

4. While the cabbage is roasting, heat the butter in a saucepan over medium-low heat. When the butter has melted, add the Buffalo sauce and whisk to combine. Add the chicken and toss to coat. Reduce the heat to low and continue warming until the cabbage has finished roasting.

5. Top each cabbage slice with ½ cup of the chicken mixture, then some of the blue cheese, celery, and green onions, if using.

CALORIES: 269 | FAT: 15g | PROTEIN: 16g | TOTAL CARBS: 9g | DIETARY FIBER: 4.2g | NET CARBS: 4.8g

Zucchini Noodles with Pesto Cream Sauce

makes 4 servings · prep time: 10 minutes (plus time to salt zucchini)
cook time: 10 minutes

I love the simplicity of this recipe. Even with only 10 minutes of cooking time, it has the rich and complex flavors of a dish that has been cooked for hours. If you would like to add more protein to it, top it with grilled chicken or even shrimp.

ingredients

2 large zucchini, spiral-sliced

2 teaspoons sea salt

For the pesto cream sauce:

¾ cup grated Parmesan cheese

½ cup heavy cream

2 tablespoons pesto

¼ teaspoon ground black pepper

For garnish:

¼ cup pine nuts

¼ cup sun-dried tomatoes, chopped

Fresh basil leaves

tip: Pine nuts are technically seeds, not nuts, so this recipe is marked as nut-free. If you have an allergy or a sensitivity to pine nuts, however, you should skip this recipe.

directions

1. Lay the zucchini noodles in a single layer on a bed of paper towels. Sprinkle the zucchini with the salt and let rest for 10 to 15 minutes. The salt will help draw out the excess moisture so that the zucchini noodles do not water down the sauce. When the noodles have released their liquid, place a layer of fresh paper towels on top and dab away the excess moisture, then set the noodles aside.

2. While the noodles are resting, make the sauce: Place the Parmesan, heavy cream, pesto, and pepper in a saucepan over medium heat. Cook, stirring frequently, until the cheese has melted and the sauce begins to thicken, about 7 minutes.

3. Add the zucchini noodles to the sauce and toss to coat. Cook for 2 to 3 minutes, until the noodles are tender but not mushy.

4. Transfer the noodles to a serving dish and top with the pine nuts, sun-dried tomatoes, and basil leaves.

CALORIES: 302 | FAT: 25g | PROTEIN: 12g | TOTAL CARBS: 9g | DIETARY FIBER: 3g | NET CARBS: 6g

Sides

Pan-Fried Brussels Sprouts with
Creamy Dijon Cider Dressing / 108

Green Onion and Lime
Cauliflower Rice / 110

Cheesy Zucchini Gratin / 112

Sautéed Asparagus with
Mushrooms and Bacon / 114

Cauliflower Steaks with
Cheesy Bacon Sauce / 116

Sautéed Green Beans with Ham / 118

Herbed Goat Cheese
Cauliflower Mash / 120

Pan-Fried Brussels Sprouts with Creamy Dijon Cider Dressing

 EGG-FREE · NUT-FREE · makes 8 servings · prep time: 10 minutes · cook time: 10 minutes

These aren't the mushy, overcooked Brussels sprouts of your childhood. At least that's how Brussels sprouts were served in my home when I was growing up. Pan-frying or oven-roasting Brussels sprouts takes away a lot of that bitter flavor profile they are known for, and mushiness is no longer an issue. Pairing the sprouts with this creamy Dijon cider dressing is a match made in heaven. Think honey mustard without the added carbs from honey. Yum!

ingredients

2 tablespoons olive oil

2 pounds fresh Brussels sprouts, quartered

Sea salt and ground black pepper

For the dressing:

½ cup full-fat sour cream

3 tablespoons Dijon mustard

1 tablespoon apple cider vinegar

2 teaspoons powdered erythritol

directions

1. Heat the olive oil in a large skillet over medium-high heat. Add the Brussels sprouts and sprinkle generously with salt and pepper. Cook until the sprouts have a nice char on all sides and are crisp-tender, about 10 minutes.

2. While the Brussels sprouts are cooking, make the dressing: In a large bowl, mix together the sour cream, Dijon mustard, vinegar, and erythritol.

3. Toss the cooked Brussels sprouts in the dressing before serving. Store leftovers in the refrigerator for up to 1 week.

tip: This dressing is also great with shaved raw Brussels sprouts as a cold salad.

CALORIES: 110 | FAT: 7g | PROTEIN: 4g | TOTAL CARBS: 10g | DIETARY FIBER: 4.5g | NET CARBS: 5.5g | ERYTHRITOL: 1.3g

Green Onion and Lime Cauliflower Rice

makes 6 servings · prep time: 10 minutes · cook time: 23 minutes

This cauliflower rice recipe is perhaps my favorite side dish in this book. It is simple yet flavorful and complements so many main dishes. I love serving it with Greek Meatballs (page 88), Fish Taco Bowls (page 92), and Shrimp Piccata (page 98). See? It goes with just about everything! I like to make a double or triple batch of this rice and freeze it in individual portions to heat up to accompany quick-and-easy weeknight dinners.

ingredients

2 tablespoons butter or olive oil

6 green onions, sliced, white and green parts separated

1 small white onion, chopped (about ½ cup)

4 cloves garlic, minced

6 cups riced cauliflower

1 tablespoon grated lime zest

Juice of ½ lime

1½ teaspoons sea salt

¼ teaspoon ground black pepper

½ cup chicken stock

Lime wedges, for serving

directions

1. Heat the butter in a large skillet over medium heat. Add the white parts of the green onions, the white onion, and the garlic and sauté until the garlic is fragrant and the onions are translucent, about 5 minutes.

2. Add the cauliflower, lime zest, lime juice, salt, and pepper. Sauté until the cauliflower is tender, about 10 minutes.

3. Add the chicken stock and cook, stirring often, for an additional 8 minutes, or until all of the stock is evaporated and the rice is tender but not mushy.

4. Mix in the green parts of the green onions and serve with lime wedges.

tips: For a delicious variation, try making this dish with cilantro in place of the green onions.

To make this dish dairy-free and Paleo compliant, use olive oil instead of butter.

CALORIES: 75 | FAT: 4g | PROTEIN: 3g | TOTAL CARBS: 7.5g | DIETARY FIBER: 2.7g | NET CARBS: 4.8g

Cheesy Zucchini Gratin

makes 8 servings · prep time: 10 minutes · cook time: 30 minutes

The sauce in this zucchini gratin reminds me of a rich gourmet mac and cheese. Making a gratin is an excellent way to repurpose leftover vegetables or to use up vegetables from your refrigerator that might be nearing the end of their freshness. This cheese sauce pairs perfectly with just about any low-carb vegetable.

ingredients

2 tablespoons butter or ghee

1 small onion, halved and thinly sliced

3 cloves garlic, minced

4 medium zucchini (about 8 inches), sliced into coins

1 teaspoon sea salt

½ teaspoon ground black pepper

¼ teaspoon ground nutmeg

For the sauce:

1 cup heavy cream

½ cup grated Parmesan cheese

2 tablespoons butter

1½ cups shredded sharp white cheddar cheese, divided

tip: Feel free to make this recipe with any type of cheese you prefer. Another one of my favorite combinations is pepper Jack and mozzarella.

directions

1. Heat the butter in a large skillet over medium heat. Add the onion and garlic and cook until the onion is translucent and the garlic is fragrant, about 5 minutes.

2. Preheat the oven to 425°F.

3. Add the zucchini, salt, pepper, and nutmeg to the skillet and cook until the zucchini is crisp-tender, about 5 minutes.

4. Meanwhile, make the sauce: Place the heavy cream, Parmesan cheese, and butter in a microwave-safe mixing bowl. Microwave until the cream is warm and the butter is melted. (Or heat the cream, cheese, and butter in a small saucepan over medium-low heat on the stovetop.)

5. Transfer half of the zucchini mixture to a 10-inch casserole dish. Top with ¾ cup of the cheddar cheese, then the remaining zucchini. Pour the cream mixture over the top, then sprinkle with the remaining ¾ cup of cheddar cheese.

6. Bake for 20 minutes, or until golden brown and bubbling on top. Store leftovers in the refrigerator for up to 1 week.

CALORIES: 285 | FAT: 25g | PROTEIN: 9g | TOTAL CARBS: 5.3g | DIETARY FIBER: 1.3g | NET CARBS: 4g

Sautéed Asparagus with Mushrooms and Bacon

NET CARBS
2.7g

makes 4 servings · prep time: 10 minutes · cook time: 20 minutes

Why discard bacon drippings when you can cook your food in them? When we make bacon, we save the rendered fat in a jar and use it for cooking veggies and eggs. Delicious!

ingredients

4 slices bacon, chopped

4 ounces mushrooms, thinly sliced

2 cloves garlic, minced

1 pound asparagus, ends trimmed

Sea salt and ground black pepper (optional)

tip: This dish is also amazing made with broccoli.

directions

1. In a large skillet over medium heat, cook the bacon until crispy. Using a slotted spoon, remove the bacon from the pan and set aside.

2. Add the mushrooms and garlic to the hot drippings in the skillet. Sauté until the mushrooms are tender and have released their liquid, about 5 minutes.

3. Add the asparagus and cooked bacon to the skillet and sauté until the asparagus is crisp-tender, about 10 minutes. Taste and season with salt and pepper, if desired.

CALORIES: 71 | FAT: 3g | PROTEIN: 7g | TOTAL CARBS: 5.5g | DIETARY FIBER: 2.8g | NET CARBS: 2.7g

Cauliflower Steaks with Cheesy Bacon Sauce

makes 6 servings · prep time: 10 minutes (not including time to cook bacon)
cook time: 25 minutes

What makes roasted cauliflower steaks even more delicious? Cheese and bacon, of course! What makes everything better? Also cheese and bacon! What did the cauliflower bank robber say to the broccoli getaway driver? Floret!

ingredients

1 large head cauliflower

2 tablespoons olive oil

Sea salt and ground black pepper

For the sauce:

¾ cup heavy cream

2 cups shredded sharp cheddar cheese

2 cloves garlic, minced

1 tablespoon Dijon mustard

1 teaspoon hot sauce

½ teaspoon sea salt

¼ teaspoon ground black pepper

8 slices bacon, cooked crisp and chopped

4 green onions, sliced

directions

1. Preheat the oven to 425°F. Line a rimmed baking sheet with parchment paper or a silicone baking mat.

2. Cut the cauliflower into 6 equal slices or "steaks," slicing from the top down through to the core. Place the cauliflower steaks in a single layer on the prepared baking sheet, drizzle with the olive oil, and then sprinkle generously with salt and pepper.

3. Roast the cauliflower steaks for 15 minutes, then flip and roast for an additional 5 to 10 minutes, until fork-tender and browned on the edges.

4. While the cauliflower is roasting, make the sauce: Place the heavy cream, cheddar cheese, garlic, Dijon mustard, hot sauce, salt, and pepper in a large saucepan over medium heat. Stir continuously until the cheese has melted and the ingredients are well incorporated, then reduce the heat to low and stir occasionally while the cauliflower finishes roasting.

5. Top the cauliflower steaks with the cheese sauce, bacon, and green onions before serving.

time-saving tip:

Batch cook bacon ahead of time so you have lots of precooked bacon for recipes like this one.

CALORIES: 332 | FAT: 29g | PROTEIN: 14g | TOTAL CARBS: 7.3g | DIETARY FIBER: 2.2g | NET CARBS: 5.1g

Sautéed Green Beans with Ham

makes 6 servings · prep time: 10 minutes · cook time: 8 minutes

With just about eight minutes of cooking time, side dishes don't get much easier than this! I'll let you in on a little secret: these green beans are fantastic with the Cheesy Bacon Sauce from the Cauliflower Steaks recipe on page 116.

ingredients

2 tablespoons olive oil

1 pound fresh green beans, trimmed

8 ounces ham, diced

1 tablespoon dried minced onions

½ teaspoon sea salt

¼ teaspoon ground black pepper

directions

1. Heat the olive oil in a large skillet over medium-high heat. When the pan is hot, add the green beans, ham, dried onions, salt, and pepper.

2. Sauté until the green beans are crisp-tender, about 8 minutes. Store leftovers in the refrigerator for up to 1 week.

CALORIES: 113 | FAT: 7g | PROTEIN: 8g | TOTAL CARBS: 6.5g | DIETARY FIBER: 2.7g | NET CARBS: 3.8g

Herbed Goat Cheese Cauliflower Mash

makes 8 servings · prep time: 15 minutes · cook time: 30 minutes

NET CARBS
4.4g

It is really hard to make a pile of cauliflower mash look pretty, but trust me when I tell you that this stuff is seriously delicious. It doesn't need gravy or any other kind of sauce; it is amazingly flavorful served just as it is. This recipe is the closest I have come to replicating the taste and texture of real mashed potatoes. It is perfect for a low-carb holiday table or just your average Tuesday night.

ingredients

1 large head cauliflower

Sea salt and ground black pepper

4 ounces fresh (soft) goat cheese

½ cup grated Parmesan cheese

½ cup heavy cream

¼ cup full-fat sour cream

¼ cup plus 2 tablespoons (¾ stick) butter, divided

3 cloves garlic, minced

2 tablespoons chopped fresh chives, plus extra for garnish

1 tablespoon chopped fresh flat-leaf parsley, plus extra for garnish

1 teaspoon chopped fresh dill weed, plus extra for garnish

Pinch of red pepper flakes (optional)

directions

1. Preheat the oven to 425°F. Line a rimmed baking sheet with parchment paper or a silicone baking mat.

2. Core the head of cauliflower and cut it into florets. Spread the florets in a single layer on the prepared baking sheet and sprinkle generously with salt and pepper.

3. Roast the cauliflower for 20 to 30 minutes, until it is tender.

4. Place the roasted cauliflower, goat cheese, Parmesan, heavy cream, sour cream, ¼ cup of the butter, garlic, chives, parsley, dill, and red pepper flakes, if using, in a food processor. Pulse until smooth and fluffy. Taste and add more salt and pepper, if desired.

5. Top the mash with the remaining 2 tablespoons of butter and extra fresh herbs before serving. Store leftovers in the refrigerator for up to 1 week.

CALORIES: 236 | FAT: 21g | PROTEIN: 8g | TOTAL CARBS: 7g | DIETARY FIBER: 2.6g | NET CARBS: 4.4g

SWEET
Treats

Chocolate Chip Cookies for Two

 makes 2 cookies (1 per serving) · prep time: 5 minutes · cook time: 20 minutes

Cookies for two: perfect for a romantic low-carb date night or for those random times you are hit with a relentless sweet tooth. It's guilt-free indulgence at its finest. I love to eat these cookies fresh out of the oven, topped with a dollop of fresh whipped cream (see page 130).

ingredients

¼ cup blanched almond flour

2 tablespoons butter, softened

2 tablespoons granular erythritol

½ teaspoon pure vanilla extract

Pinch of sea salt

2 tablespoons sugar-free dark chocolate chips

directions

1. Preheat the oven to 350°F. Lightly grease two 4-inch ramekins.

2. Place the almond flour, butter, erythritol, vanilla extract, and salt in a small mixing bowl. Mix by hand until the ingredients are well incorporated. Fold in the chocolate chips.

3. Divide the batter equally between the ramekins, then place the ramekins on a rimmed baking sheet for stability. Bake for 20 minutes, or until golden brown on top. Serve in the ramekins and eat with a spoon.

CALORIES: 207 | FAT: 21g | PROTEIN: 4g | TOTAL CARBS: 6g | DIETARY FIBER: 3.5g | NET CARBS: 2.5g | ERYTHRITOL: 15g

Mini Blueberry Cheesecakes

NET CARBS
4.5g

makes 12 mini cheesecakes (1 per serving) · prep time: 10 minutes · cook time: 30 minutes

These low-carb cheesecakes are incredibly easy to whip up and will satisfy your sweet tooth. The fact that they are mini-sized makes practicing portion control a lot easier. Well, it's easier to see what an exact portion is, anyway. What you choose to do with that information is up to you.

ingredients

For the crust:

1 cup blanched almond flour

1 tablespoon brown sugar erythritol (see tips)

¼ cup (½ stick) salted butter, melted

For the filling:

2 (8-ounce) packages full-fat cream cheese, softened

2 large eggs

2 teaspoons pure lemon extract

1 teaspoon pure vanilla extract

½ cup granular erythritol

For the topping:

1 cup frozen blueberries

tips: If you do not have brown sugar erythritol, you can substitute granular erythritol or omit it altogether.

For best results, make these cheesecakes a day ahead of time and refrigerate for 24 hours before serving.

directions

1. Preheat the oven to 350°F. Line a standard-size 12-well metal muffin pan with paper liners or use a silicone muffin pan.

2. In a medium mixing bowl, combine the almond flour and brown sugar erythritol. Add the melted butter and mix until the flour is coated and has the texture of wet sand.

3. Divide the mixture evenly among the 12 wells of the muffin pan and use a spoon to press it into an even layer. Par-bake the crusts for 5 minutes.

4. While the crusts are baking, make the filling: Place the cream cheese in a large mixing bowl. Using an electric hand mixer, beat the cream cheese until fluffy.

5. Add the eggs, lemon extract, vanilla extract, and granular erythritol to the bowl with the cream cheese and mix until the ingredients are well combined and the mixture is smooth, scraping down the sides of the bowl with a rubber spatula as needed.

6. Divide the cheesecake mixture evenly among the 12 wells of the muffin pan. If using a silicone pan, place it on top of a rimmed baking sheet.

7. Bake the cheesecakes for 25 minutes, or until they are set. They will still be a little jiggly in the center.

8. While the cheesecakes are baking, heat the blueberries in a small saucepan over medium-low heat. Let simmer for 15 minutes. Mash the berries slightly to release their juices and allow the juices to thicken. Let cool.

9. Once the cheesecakes and blueberries have cooled, top each cheesecake with the blueberries. Store leftovers in the refrigerator for up to 1 week.

CALORIES: 233 | FAT: 21g | PROTEIN: 6g | TOTAL CARBS: 6.5g | DIETARY FIBER: 2g | NET CARBS: 4.5g | ERYTHRITOL: 13g

Double Chocolate Flourless Brownies

makes 16 brownies (1 per serving) · prep time: 10 minutes · cook time: 25 minutes

Who doesn't love a chewy, fudgy brownie? Certainly no one I have ever met. Brownies always have been, and still are, my favorite dessert. I love those crispy edge pieces. When I was little, I was known to sneak into the kitchen and cut around the entire perimeter of the brownie pan in order to eat all of the edges before anyone else could get to them. Who am I kidding? I still do that!

ingredients

1 cup natural creamy almond butter

⅔ cup powdered erythritol

2 tablespoons unsweetened cocoa powder

2 tablespoons peanut butter powder (see tip)

2 large eggs

2 tablespoons water

1 tablespoon salted butter, melted

1½ teaspoons pure vanilla extract

1 teaspoon baking soda

¼ cup sugar-free dark chocolate chips

directions

1. Preheat the oven to 350°F. Lightly grease an 8-inch square baking dish. Alternatively, you can line it with parchment paper, leaving a couple inches of overhang on the sides for easy removal.

2. Place the almond butter, erythritol, cocoa powder, peanut butter powder, eggs, water, melted butter, vanilla extract, and baking soda in a large mixing bowl. Using an electric hand mixer, mix until the ingredients are well combined. Fold in the chocolate chips.

3. Pour the batter into the prepared baking dish and spread in an even layer. Bake for 20 to 25 minutes, until the center is set.

4. Let cool in the pan for 15 minutes before cutting into 16 squares and serving. Store leftovers in an airtight container in the pantry or on the counter for up to 1 week.

tip: If you can't find peanut butter powder at your local grocery store, you can get it on Amazon. Buying it online will likely save you a few dollars.

CALORIES: 129 | FAT: 11g | PROTEIN: 5g | TOTAL CARBS: 4.3g | DIETARY FIBER: 2.8g | NET CARBS: 1.5g | ERYTHRITOL: 9.4g

Lemon Mousse

 NUT-FREE makes 6 servings · prep time: 15 minutes · cook time: 6 minutes

I am a huge fan of lemon-flavored desserts. I love the bright, refreshing acidity of fresh lemon juice. This mousse is the perfect palate cleanser. It is light and fluffy while still tasting incredibly decadent.

ingredients

⅔ cup granular erythritol

1 tablespoon grated lemon zest, plus extra for garnish

⅓ cup fresh lemon juice

2 large egg yolks

½ cup mascarpone cheese

½ cup full-fat sour cream

For the whipped cream:

1 cup heavy cream

1 tablespoon powdered erythritol

½ teaspoon pure vanilla extract

For garnish (optional):

Slivered almonds

Fresh mint leaves

directions

1. Set up a double boiler by placing a heatproof bowl on top of a saucepan filled with about 1 inch of water. Make sure that the bowl is suspended above the water line and is not touching the water. Bring the water to a simmer.

2. Place the granular erythritol, lemon zest, lemon juice, and egg yolks in the bowl and whisk to combine. Continue whisking until the sweetener has dissolved and the mixture has thickened, about 6 minutes.

3. Remove the bowl from the heat and let the mixture cool slightly. Mix in the mascarpone and sour cream. Place the bowl in the refrigerator while you make the whipped cream.

4. Make the whipped cream: Place the heavy cream, powdered erythritol, and vanilla extract in a large mixing bowl. Using an electric hand mixer or a stand mixer, whip the cream until it is light and fluffy with stiff peaks. The cream will double in volume when whipped.

5. Remove the lemon mixture from the fridge and fold in 1½ cups of the whipped cream.

6. Divide the lemon mousse among 6 serving cups. Top the mousse with the remaining whipped cream and extra lemon zest. Garnish with almonds and mint, if desired.

CALORIES: 240 | FAT: 24g | PROTEIN: 3g | TOTAL CARBS: 3.3g | DIETARY FIBER: 0.2g | NET CARBS: 3.1g | ERYTHRITOL: 25g

Sesame Shortbread Sugar Cookies

 EGG-FREE

makes 24 cookies (2 per serving) · prep time: 10 minutes · cook time: 16 minutes

Move over, peanut butter; your older, more refined cousin, tahini, is in the house. Not only is tahini delicious, but it is a great option for those with a peanut allergy. Tahini is made by grinding toasted sesame seeds into a paste. It is commonly found in Mediterranean dishes and has a place in both sweet and savory recipes. These soft and chewy sesame cookies are the perfect textural blend of shortbread meets sugar cookie.

ingredients

2½ cups blanched almond flour

2 teaspoons baking powder

½ teaspoon sea salt

¾ cup (1½ sticks) butter, softened

1 cup granular erythritol

2 teaspoons pure vanilla extract

¾ cup tahini

¼ cup toasted sesame seeds

directions

1. Place oven racks in the upper and lower thirds of the oven and preheat the oven to 350°F. Line two baking sheets with parchment paper or silicone baking mats.

2. Whisk together the almond flour, baking powder, and salt in a medium mixing bowl and set aside.

3. Place the butter, erythritol, and vanilla extract in a large mixing bowl. Using an electric hand mixer, beat until light and fluffy, about 3 minutes.

4. Beat the tahini into the wet ingredients, then add the dry ingredients a little at a time, beating after each addition.

5. Using a large spoon, scoop up heaping mounds of the dough (about 2 tablespoons each) and drop them onto the prepared baking sheets, spacing the mounds about 2 inches apart. Sprinkle each mound with ½ teaspoon of sesame seeds.

6. Bake for 16 minutes, rotating the baking sheets halfway through. The cookies will be soft in the center and golden brown around the edges. Let them cool on the baking sheets before serving; they will continue to firm up as they cool. Store leftovers in an airtight container in the pantry or on the counter for up to 1 week.

CALORIES: 340 | FAT: 32g | PROTEIN: 8g | TOTAL CARBS: 8.8g | DIETARY FIBER: 3.8g | NET CARBS: 5g | ERYTHRITOL: 20g

Pumpkin Cheesecake Mousse

makes 10 servings (½ cup per serving) · prep time: 15 minutes

This mousse has all the flavors of pumpkin pie but a deliciously creamy whipped texture. It is sure to become a fall favorite. I like to top mine with a little fresh whipped cream (see page 130) and a sprinkle of pumpkin pie spice. Easy and delicious!

ingredients

12 ounces full-fat cream cheese (1½ cups), softened

1 (15-ounce) can unsweetened pumpkin puree

½ cup powdered erythritol

2 tablespoons pumpkin pie spice

¾ cup heavy cream

2 teaspoons pure vanilla extract

tip: This mousse is great right away, but for a thicker consistency, you can chill it before serving.

directions

1. Place the cream cheese and pumpkin puree in a large mixing bowl. Using an electric hand mixer, mix until smooth and creamy with no visible clumps.

2. Add the erythritol, pumpkin pie spice, heavy cream, and vanilla extract and mix until the ingredients are well incorporated. Store leftovers in the refrigerator for up to 1 week.

CALORIES: 215 | FAT: 18g | PROTEIN: 3g | TOTAL CARBS: 3g | DIETARY FIBER: 1g | NET CARBS: 2g | ERYTHRITOL: 12g

Avocado Chocolate Pudding

**NET CARBS
4g**

DAIRY-FREE · EGG-FREE · NUT-FREE

makes 4 servings · prep time: 10 minutes

I love to sneak healthy real-food ingredients into everyday sweet treats. It is rewarding to know that I can still enjoy the occasional dessert while keeping it healthy and sticking to my whole-food, low-carb lifestyle.

ingredients

2 medium avocados, peeled, pitted, and diced

½ cup unsweetened cocoa powder

¼ cup coconut milk (see tips)

¼ cup powdered erythritol

2 teaspoons pure vanilla extract

Pinch of sea salt

¼ cup sugar-free dark chocolate chips (optional)

tips: This recipe can be made with almond milk or heavy cream in place of the coconut milk.

For the best taste, refrigerate the pudding for at least an hour before serving.

directions

Place the avocados, cocoa powder, coconut milk, erythritol, vanilla extract, and salt in a food processor and pulse until smooth and creamy. Serve the pudding topped with the chocolate chips, if desired.

CALORIES: 147 | FAT: 13g | PROTEIN: 4g | TOTAL CARBS: 13g | DIETARY FIBER: 9g | NET CARBS: 4g | ERYTHRITOL: 15g

Basics

Taco Seasoning

makes ½ cup (2 tablespoons per serving) · prep time: 5 minutes

Making your own seasoning blends at home is quick and easy, not to mention better for you. It will likely save you money as well. There are a lot of unnecessary additives in store-bought seasoning packets.

ingredients

3 tablespoons chili powder

3 tablespoons ground cumin

1 tablespoon plus 1 teaspoon celery salt

1 tablespoon plus 1 teaspoon garlic powder

1 tablespoon onion powder

¾ teaspoon ground black pepper

½ teaspoon cayenne pepper

tip: To make taco meat, simply brown the ground beef, ground turkey, or other meat of choice, then drain the excess grease. Add ⅔ cup of water and ¼ cup of taco seasoning per pound of meat, reduce the heat to low, and let simmer for 5 minutes, or until thickened.

directions

Mix together all of the ingredients and place in an airtight container. Store in the spice cabinet for up to 3 months.

CALORIES: 46 | FAT: 2g | PROTEIN: 2g | TOTAL CARBS: 8g | DIETARY FIBER: 3g | NET CARBS: 5g

Roasted Tomatillo Salsa Verde

NET CARBS
1.5g

makes 2 cups (2 tablespoons per serving) · prep time: 10 minutes
cook time: 7 minutes

Salsa verde is one of my favorite condiments. I always keep a fresh batch of it in the re-frigerator. My favorite way to eat it is on my morning eggs.

ingredients

1 pound tomatillos, destemmed and husked

½ small red onion, cut into large chunks

4 cloves garlic, peeled

2 tablespoons olive oil

1 serrano pepper, minced

1 tablespoon chopped fresh cilantro

2 teaspoons fresh lime juice

1½ teaspoons sea salt

1 teaspoon ground cumin

½ cup chicken stock

directions

1. Preheat the oven to broil-high. Line a rimmed baking sheet with parchment paper or a silicone baking mat.

2. Slice the tomatillos in half and place cut side down on the prepared baking sheet, along with the onion and garlic. Drizzle with the olive oil.

3. Broil for 5 to 7 minutes, until the tomatillos are slightly charred and begin to blister.

4. Place the roasted tomatillos, onion, and garlic in a blender or food processor, along with the serrano pepper, cilantro, lime juice, salt, and cumin. Pulse until pureed.

5. Add the chicken stock and pulse a few times to mix it in. Store in the refrigerator for up to 2 weeks.

CALORIES: 11 | FAT: 0.3g | PROTEIN: 0.3g | TOTAL CARBS: 2g | DIETARY FIBER: 0.5g | NET CARBS: 1.5g

Greek Feta Dressing

 makes 2 cups (2 tablespoons per serving) · prep time: 5 minutes

Not only is this dressing good on Greek Salad (page 50), but it also makes a terrific marinade for chicken or fish. For a quick-and-easy weeknight meal, place 2 pounds of chicken or fish and a batch of this dressing in a large freezer-safe storage bag and store in the freezer. Then, when you are ready to eat it, you can simply thaw it and toss the meat and marinade in a slow cooker or bake it in the oven. Dinner doesn't get much simpler than that.

ingredients

1 cup light olive oil or avocado oil

½ cup red wine vinegar

Juice of 1 small lemon

4 cloves garlic, minced

1 tablespoon Dijon mustard

½ teaspoon sea salt

¼ teaspoon ground black pepper

¼ cup crumbled feta cheese

tip: This dressing is also amazing with chopped Kalamata olives stirred in at the end along with the feta cheese.

directions

Place the oil, vinegar, lemon juice, garlic, Dijon mustard, salt, and pepper in a blender or food processor and pulse until well combined. Stir in the feta cheese. Store in the refrigerator for up to 2 weeks.

CALORIES: 129 | FAT: 14g | PROTEIN: 4g | TOTAL CARBS: 0.5g | DIETARY FIBER: 0g | NET CARBS: 0.5g

Citrus Vinaigrette

makes 1¼ cups (2 tablespoons per serving) · prep time: 10 minutes

ingredients

¾ cup light olive oil or avocado oil

¼ cup red wine vinegar

3 tablespoons fresh lemon juice

3 tablespoons fresh lime juice

3 tablespoons fresh orange juice

1 clove garlic, minced

1 tablespoon powdered erythritol (optional)

1 teaspoon Dijon mustard

¼ teaspoon sea salt

¼ teaspoon ground black pepper

tip: To make this dressing Paleo compliant, omit the erythritol.

directions

Place all of the ingredients in a blender or food processor and pulse until well combined. Store in the refrigerator for up to 2 weeks.

CALORIES: 161 | FAT: 17g | PROTEIN: 0.7g | TOTAL CARBS: 1.8g | DIETARY FIBER: 0g | NET CARBS: 1.8g

Avocado Ranch Dressing

 makes 2½ cups (2 tablespoons per serving) · prep time: 10 minutes

This low-carb ranch dressing is a staple in my home. We use it as a dip for fresh veggies, as a salad dressing, and even over grilled fish, like in the Fish Taco Bowls (page 92). The healthy fat boost from the avocado makes it the perfect keto dressing. It takes traditional ranch to a whole new level.

ingredients

1 medium avocado, peeled and pitted

½ cup mayonnaise

½ cup full-fat sour cream

½ cup water

1 clove garlic, minced

1 tablespoon chopped fresh flat-leaf parsley

1 tablespoon chopped fresh chives

1½ teaspoons chopped fresh dill weed

2 teaspoons apple cider vinegar

½ teaspoon onion powder

¼ teaspoon sea salt

⅛ teaspoon ground black pepper

directions

Place all of the ingredients in a blender or food processor and pulse until smooth and creamy. Store in the refrigerator for up to 1 week.

CALORIES: 61 | FAT: 6g | PROTEIN: 4g | TOTAL CARBS: 1g | DIETARY FIBER: 0.5g | NET CARBS: 0.5g

Strawberry Balsamic Vinaigrette

DAIRY-FREE · EGG-FREE · NUT-FREE · PALEO

makes 1¼ cups (2 tablespoons per serving) · prep time: 10 minutes

Fresh, light, and super easy to make—this is my kind of dressing! If this vinaigrette is thicker than you like it, slowly add water as you blend it to get it to the consistency you prefer.

ingredients

½ cup light olive oil or avocado oil

⅓ cup sliced strawberries

¼ cup balsamic vinegar

1 tablespoon plus 1 teaspoon Dijon mustard

1 tablespoon fresh lemon juice

1 clove garlic, minced

1 small shallot, minced

½ teaspoon sea salt

⅛ teaspoon ground black pepper

Pinch of red pepper flakes

directions

Place all of the ingredients in a blender or food processor and pulse until well blended and smooth. Store in the refrigerator for up to 2 weeks.

CALORIES: 106 | FAT: 11g | PROTEIN: 0.1g | TOTAL CARBS: 1.6g | DIETARY FIBER: 0.1g | NET CARBS: 1.5g

Cucumber Sauce

 NUT-FREE makes 1½ cups (2 tablespoons per serving) · prep time: 10 minutes

This cucumber sauce is super simple to make and uses basic ingredients that you probably already have in your refrigerator. It pairs perfectly with Mediterranean flavors and just about everything else, too—chicken, fish, beef, you name it! It makes a terrific salad dressing and even complements dishes like Greek Meatballs (page 88) and Fish Taco Bowls (page 92).

ingredients

1 mini seedless cucumber, sliced

½ cup full-fat sour cream

¼ cup mayonnaise

2 tablespoons fresh lemon juice

2 tablespoons chopped fresh chives

1 tablespoon chopped fresh dill weed

2 cloves garlic, minced

½ teaspoon sea salt

¼ teaspoon ground black pepper

directions

Place all of the ingredients in a blender or food processor and pulse until smooth and creamy. Store in the refrigerator for up to 2 weeks.

CALORIES: 53 | FAT: 5g | PROTEIN: 0.4g | TOTAL CARBS: 1.2g | DIETARY FIBER: 0g | NET CARBS: 1.2g

Barbecue Sauce

 EGG-FREE   NUT-FREE   makes 1 cup (2 tablespoons per serving) · prep time: 5 minutes
cook time: 15 minutes

Barbecue sauce seems to be one of the first condiments to go when people switch to a low-carb lifestyle. That is because traditional barbecue sauce recipes and store-bought brands are loaded with sugar. Well, I am putting barbecue sauce back on the low-carb table!

ingredients

1 cup tomato sauce

2 tablespoons powdered erythritol

1 tablespoon salted butter

2 teaspoons apple cider vinegar

2 teaspoons onion powder

1½ teaspoons liquid smoke

1 teaspoon fresh lemon juice

1 clove garlic, minced

¼ teaspoon sea salt

¼ teaspoon ground black pepper

tip: For a more molasses-flavored barbecue sauce, use 1 tablespoon of brown sugar erythritol instead of the powdered erythritol.

directions

1. Combine all of the ingredients in a saucepan over medium heat and simmer for 15 minutes.

2. Taste and add more salt, if desired. Store in the refrigerator for up to 1 week.

CALORIES: 39 | FAT: 3g | PROTEIN: 0.6g | TOTAL CARBS: 2.8g | DIETARY FIBER: 0.6g | NET CARBS: 2.2g | ERYTHRITOL: 4g

Easy Peasy Blender Hollandaise

 NUT-FREE · makes 1 cup (2 tablespoons per serving) · prep time: 5 minutes

In my book, hollandaise is the perfect keto condiment. It is high in fat and tastes good on just about everything—equally good over eggs as it is over a perfectly grilled, juicy steak. It is also amazing over roasted vegetables and on salmon.

ingredients

4 large egg yolks

2 tablespoons fresh lemon juice

Pinch of mustard powder

Dash of hot sauce

½ cup (1 stick) salted butter, melted

tip: To reheat this hollandaise and prevent the eggs from scrambling, heat it in the microwave on 30 percent power in 30-second intervals.

directions

1. Place the egg yolks, lemon juice, mustard powder, and hot sauce in a blender. Pulse until the ingredients are well combined.

2. Turn the blender to high and slowly pour in the melted butter. Blend until the sauce is thick, about 30 seconds. Store in the refrigerator for up to 2 weeks.

CALORIES: 130 | FAT: 14g | PROTEIN: 2g | TOTAL CARBS: 0.8g | DIETARY FIBER: 0g | NET CARBS: 0.8g

Allergen Index

RECIPES	PAGE	DAIRY-FREE	EGG-FREE	NUT-FREE	PALEO
Buffalo Chicken Dip	32		✓	✓	
Mediterranean Flatbread	34				
Dill Pickle Deviled Eggs	36	✓		✓	✓
Buttery Garlic Crescent Rolls	38				
Tahini Ranch Dip	40	✓	✓	✓	✓
Pico de Gallo	41	✓	✓	✓	✓
Cheddar Jalapeño Bacon Biscuits	42				
Strawberry Spinach Salad	46		✓		
Shaved Brussels Sprouts and Kale Salad	48		✓		
Greek Salad	50		✓	✓	
Taco Wedge Salad	52		✓	✓	
Cucumber Dill Tuna Salad	54	✓		✓	✓
Barbecue Chicken Mockaroni Salad	56			✓	
Fortune Cookie Waffles	60			✓	
Ham and Spinach Eggs Benedict	62			✓	
Cheesy Pico Eggs	64			✓	
Sausage Balls	66				
Sour Cream and Chive Egg Clouds	68			✓	
Ham and Cheese Waffles	70			✓	
Chicken Cordon Bleu Frittata	72			✓	
Pork Chops with Herbed Goat Cheese Butter	76		✓	✓	
Spicy Sausage and Cabbage Stir-Fry	78	✓	✓	✓	✓
Zucchini Noodles with Hamburger Gravy	80		✓	✓	
Chicken Sausage and Vegetable Skillet	82	✓	✓	✓	✓
Sloppy Joe–Stuffed Peppers	84	✓	✓	✓	
Cheesy Salsa Verde Chicken Casserole	86		✓	✓	
Greek Meatballs	88			✓	
Grilled New York Strip Steak with Blue Cheese Dijon Cream Sauce	90		✓	✓	
Fish Taco Bowls	92	✓	✓	✓	✓
Herbed Chicken with Mushrooms	94	✓	✓	✓	✓
Skillet Chicken Parmesan	96		✓	✓	
Shrimp Piccata	98		✓	✓	
Salisbury Steak	100	✓		✓	
Buffalo Chicken Roasted Cabbage Steaks	102		✓	✓	
Zucchini Noodles with Pesto Cream Sauce	104		✓	✓	
Pan-Fried Brussels Sprouts with Creamy Dijon Cider Dressing	108		✓	✓	
Green Onion and Lime Cauliflower Rice	110	✓	✓	✓	✓
Cheesy Zucchini Gratin	112		✓	✓	
Sautéed Asparagus with Mushrooms and Bacon	114	✓	✓	✓	✓
Cauliflower Steaks with Cheesy Bacon Sauce	116		✓	✓	
Sautéed Green Beans with Ham	118	✓	✓	✓	✓
Herbed Goat Cheese Cauliflower Mash	120		✓	✓	
Chocolate Chip Cookies for Two	124		✓		
Mini Blueberry Cheesecakes	126				
Double Chocolate Flourless Brownies	128				
Lemon Mousse	130			✓	
Sesame Shortbread Sugar Cookies	132		✓		
Pumpkin Cheesecake Mousse	134		✓	✓	
Avocado Chocolate Pudding	135	✓	✓	✓	
Taco Seasoning	138	✓	✓	✓	✓
Roasted Tomatillo Salsa Verde	139	✓	✓	✓	✓
Greek Feta Dressing	140		✓	✓	
Citrus Vinaigrette	141	✓	✓	✓	✓
Avocado Ranch Dressing	142			✓	
Strawberry Balsamic Vinaigrette	143	✓	✓	✓	✓
Cucumber Sauce	144			✓	
Barbecue Sauce	145		✓	✓	
Easy Peasy Blender Hollandaise	146			✓	

Recipe Thumbnail Index

STARTERS AND SNACKS

Buffalo Chicken
Dip

Mediterranean
Flatbread

Dill Pickle
Deviled Eggs

Buttery Garlic
Crescent Rolls

Tahini Ranch Dip

Pico de Gallo

Cheddar Jalapeño
Bacon Biscuits

SALADS

Strawberry
Spinach Salad

Shaved Brussels
Sprouts and
Kale Salad

Greek Salad

Taco Wedge
Salad

Cucumber Dill
Tuna Salad

Barbecue
Chicken
Mockaroni Salad

BREAKFAST

Fortune Cookie Waffles
60

Ham and Spinach Eggs Benedict
62

Cheesy Pico Eggs
64

Sausage Balls
66

Sour Cream and Chive Egg Clouds
68

Ham and Cheese Waffles
70

Chicken Cordon Bleu Frittata
72

LUNCH AND DINNER

Pork Chops with Herbed Goat Cheese Butter
76

Spicy Sausage and Cabbage Stir-Fry
78

Zucchini Noodles with Hamburger Gravy
80

Chicken Sausage and Vegetable Skillet
82

Sloppy Joe–Stuffed Peppers
84

Cheesy Salsa Verde Chicken Casserole
86

Greek Meatballs
88

Grilled New York Strip Steak with Blue Cheese Dijon Cream Sauce
90

Fish Taco Bowls
92

Herbed Chicken with Mushrooms
94

LUNCH AND DINNER (CONTINUED)

96

Skillet Chicken
Parmesan

98

Shrimp Piccata

100

Salisbury Steak

102

Buffalo Chicken
Roasted Cabbage
Steaks

104

Zucchini Noodles
with Pesto
Cream Sauce

SIDES

108

Pan-Fried
Brussels Sprouts
with Creamy Dijon
Cider Dressing

110

Green Onion
and Lime
Cauliflower Rice

112

Cheesy Zucchini
Gratin

114

Sautéed
Asparagus with
Mushrooms
and Bacon

116

Cauliflower Steaks
with Cheesy
Bacon Sauce

118

Sautéed Green
Beans with Ham

120

Herbed
Goat Cheese
Cauliflower Mash

SWEET TREATS

124

Chocolate Chip
Cookies for Two

126

Mini Blueberry
Cheesecakes

128

Double Chocolate
Flourless
Brownies

130

Lemon Mousse

132

Sesame
Shortbread
Sugar Cookies

134

Pumpkin
Cheesecake
Mousse

135

Avocado
Chocolate
Pudding

BASICS

138

Taco Seasoning

139

Roasted
Tomatillo
Salsa Verde

140

Greek Feta
Dressing

141

Citrus
Vinaigrette

142

Avocado Ranch
Dressing

143

Strawberry
Balsamic
Vinaigrette

144

Cucumber Sauce

145

Barbecue Sauce

146

Easy Peasy
Blender
Hollandaise

Index

Herbed Chicken with Mushrooms, 94–95
Salisbury Steak, 100–101
Sautéed Asparagus with Mushrooms and
Bacon, 114–115
Spicy Sausage and Cabbage Stir-Fry, 78–79

N
Nutiva brand, 9

O
olives
Fish Taco Bowls, 92–93
Greek Feta Dressing, 140
Greek Salad, 50–51
Mediterranean Flatbread, 34–35
Taco Wedge Salad, 52–53
onions
Barbecue Chicken Mockaroni Salad, 56–57
Cheesy Zucchini Gratin, 112–113
Chicken Sausage and Vegetable Skillet, 82–83
Greek Meatballs, 88–89
Greek Salad, 50–51
Green Onion and Lime Cauliflower Rice,
110–111
Mediterranean Flatbread, 34–35
Pico de Gallo, 41
Roasted Tomatillo Salsa Verde, 139
Salisbury Steak, 100–101
Sautéed Green Beans with Ham, 118–119
Sloppy Joe–Stuffed Peppers, 84–85
Strawberry Spinach Salad, 46–47
Zucchini Noodles with Hamburger Gravy,
80–81
oranges
Citrus Vinaigrette, 141
organizational tips and tricks, 11–13
ovenproof skillets, 16

P
Pan-Fried Brussels Sprouts with Creamy
Dijon Cider Dressing recipe, 108–109
Parmesan cheese
Cheesy Zucchini Gratin, 112–113
Herbed Goat Cheese Cauliflower Mash,
120–121
Sausage Balls, 66–67

Skillet Chicken Parmesan, 96–97
Zucchini Noodles with Hamburger Gravy,
80–81
Zucchini Noodles with Pesto Cream Sauce,
104–105
pastured eggs, 10
peaceloveandlowcarb.com (website), 96
peanut butter powder, 128
pecans
Shaved Brussels Sprouts and Kale Salad,
48–49
Pederson's Natural Farms brand, 8
pepper Jack cheese
Cheesy Zucchini Gratin, 112–113
pesto
Mediterranean Flatbread, 34–35
Zucchini Noodles with Pesto Cream Sauce,
104–105
Pico de Gallo recipe, 41
Cheesy Pico Eggs, 64–65
Cheesy Salsa Verde Chicken Casserole, 86–87
pine nuts
Zucchini Noodles with Pesto Cream Sauce,
104–105
pork. *See also* bacon
Greek Meatballs, 88–89
Pork Chops with Herbed Goat Cheese
Butter, 76–77
Pork Chops with Herbed Goat Cheese Butter
recipe, 76–77
prep containers, 16
pressure cookers, 12, 15
products, used in this book, 8–10
Pumpkin Cheesecake Mousse recipe, 134

R
refrigerating pudding, 135
reheating
biscuits, 42
hollandaise sauce, 146
repurposing leftovers, 18–19
Roasted Tomatillo Salsa Verde recipe, 139
Cheesy Pico Eggs, 64–65
romaine lettuce
Greek Salad, 50–51
rotisserie chicken, 32, 72

storing cheesecakes, 126
strawberries
    Strawberry Balsamic Vinaigrette, 143
    Strawberry Spinach Salad, 46–47
Strawberry Balsamic Vinaigrette recipe, 143
Strawberry Spinach Salad recipe, 46–47
sugar-free dark chocolate chips, 10
Swerve, 9
Swiss cheese
    Chicken Cordon Bleu Frittata, 72–73

T

Taco Seasoning recipe, 138
    Fish Taco Bowls, 92–93
Taco Wedge Salad recipe, 52–53
tacos, 19. *See also* Fish Taco Bowls recipe
tahini
    Sesame Shortbread Sugar Cookies, 132–133
    Tahini Ranch Dip, 40
Tahini Ranch Dip recipe, 40
tips and tricks, time-saving, 11–14
tomatillos
    Roasted Tomatillo Salsa Verde, 139
tomato sauce
    Barbecue Sauce, 145
    Sloppy Joe–Stuffed Peppers, 84–85
tomatoes
    Chicken Cordon Bleu Frittata, 72–73
    Fish Taco Bowls, 92–93
    Greek Salad, 50–51
    Ham and Spinach Eggs Benedict, 62–63
    Mediterranean Flatbread, 34–35
    Pico de Gallo, 41
    Taco Wedge Salad, 52–53
    Zucchini Noodles with Pesto Cream Sauce, 104–105
tools, time-saving, 15–17
Trader Joe's, 9
tuna
    Cucumber Dill Tuna Salad, 54–55

U–V

utensils, 12
vegetables, frozen, 13. *See also specific types of vegetables*

W

waffles, freezing, 60, 70
walnuts
    Strawberry Spinach Salad, 46–47
wraps, 19

Z

zucchini
    Cheesy Zucchini Gratin, 112–113
    Chicken Sausage and Vegetable Skillet, 82–83
    Zucchini Noodles with Hamburger Gravy, 80–81
    Zucchini Noodles with Pesto Cream Sauce, 104–105
Zucchini Noodles with Hamburger Gravy recipe, 80–81
Zucchini Noodles with Pesto Cream Sauce recipe, 104–105

Kyndra Holley is the face behind the keyboard at *Peace, Love and Low Carb*. What started as a hobby blog and personal weight-loss journal now gets nearly 2 million page views per month. Kyndra's focus is on easy-to-make low-carb and gluten-free comfort food, and through her recipes and candid stories of her own struggles with weight, she has helped thousands of people lose weight and live healthier lives. Her previous publications include *Keto Happy Hour, Craveable Keto Cookbook, The Primal Low Carb Kitchen Cookbook,* and several other self-published works, as well as low-carb and gluten-free meal plans.

Kyndra's mission is to show people that a low-carb lifestyle is anything but restrictive and boring. When she is not in the kitchen working her food magic, she can often be found traveling the world with her partner in crime and husband, Jon, lifting weights, doing yoga, or playing with her five crazy pups. Kyndra resides in the beautiful Pacific Northwest, just outside of Seattle, Washington. For more of her recipes, visit peaceloveandlowcarb.com.